Media Track List

Audio and video can be found in the *Inside Listening and Speaking* D
Go to www.insidelisteningandspeaking.com. Click on the Video Cente
Click on the Audio Center and choose to stream or download ⬇ the

UNIT 1

Listening	Listen		ILS_L4_U1_Listen1
	Listen for Main Ideas		ILS_L4_U1_Listen1
	Apply B		ILS_L4_U1_Listen_ApplyB
Speaking	Listen		ILS_L4_U1_Listen2
	Listen for Main Ideas		ILS_L4_U1_Listen2
	Apply A		ILS_L4_U1_Present_ApplyA
Pronunciation	Learn A		ILS_L4_U1_Pron_LearnA
	Learn B		ILS_L4_U1_Pron_LearnA
	Learn C		ILS_L4_U1_Pron_LearnC
	Apply A		ILS_L4_U1_Pron_LearnC
	Apply B		ILS_L4_U1_Pron_ApplyB
End of Unit Task A			ILS_L4_U1_End

UNIT 2

Listening	Watch		ILS_L4_U2_Watch
	Listen for Main Ideas		ILS_L4_U2_Watch
	Apply A		ILS_L4_U2_Note_ApplyA
	Apply D		ILS_L4_U2_Watch
Speaking	Listen		ILS_L4_U2_Listen
	Listen for Main Ideas		ILS_L4_U2_Listen
	Apply A		ILS_L4_U2_Present_ApplyA
Pronunciation	Learn A		ILS_L4_U2_Pron_LearnA
	Learn B		ILS_L4_U2_Pron_LearnB
	Apply A		ILS_L4_U2_Pron_ApplyA
	Apply C		ILS_L4_U2_Pron_ApplyC

UNIT 3

Listening	Listen		ILS_L4_U3_Listen1
	Listen for Main Ideas		ILS_L4_U3_Listen1
	Apply A		ILS_L4_U3_Listen1
Speaking	Listen		ILS_L4_U3_Listen2
	Listen for Main Ideas		ILS_L4_U3_Listen2
	Apply B		ILS_L4_U3_Listen2
Pronunciation	Learn A		ILS_L4_U3_Pron_LearnA
	Learn B		ILS_L4_U3_Pron_LearnB
	Learn C		ILS_L4_U3_Pron_LearnC
	Learn D		ILS_L4_U3_Pron_LearnD
	Apply A		ILS_L4_U3_Pron_ApplyA

UNIT 4

Listening	Listen		ILS_L4_U4_Listen
	Listen for Main Ideas		ILS_L4_U4_Listen
	Apply C		ILS_L4_U4_Listen_ApplyC
	Apply D		ILS_L4_U4_Listen_ApplyD
Speaking	Watch		ILS_L4_U4_Watch
	Listen for Main Ideas		ILS_L4_U4_Watch
	Apply A		ILS_L4_U4_Present_ApplyA
Pronunciation	Learn A		ILS_L4_U4_Pron_LearnA
	Learn B		ILS_L4_U4_Pron_LearnB
	Learn C		ILS_L4_U4_Pron_LearnC
	Apply A		ILS_L4_U4_Pron_ApplyA
End of Unit Task A			ILS_L4_U4_End

UNIT 5

Listening	Listen		ILS_L4_U5_Listen
	Listen for Main Ideas		ILS_L4_U5_Listen
	Apply B		ILS_L4_U5_Listen_ApplyB
Speaking	Watch		ILS_L4_U5_Watch
	Listen for Main Ideas		ILS_L4_U5_Watch
	Apply A		ILS_L4_U5_Watch
Pronunciation	Learn A		ILS_L4_U5_Pron_LearnA
	Learn B		ILS_L4_U5_Pron_LearnB

UNIT 6

Listening	Watch		ILS_L4_U6_Watch
	Listen for Main Ideas		ILS_L4_U6_Watch
	Apply A		ILS_L4_U6_Listen_ApplyA
	Apply B		ILS_L4_U6_Listen_ApplyB
Speaking	Listen		ILS_L4_U6_Listen
	Listen for Main Ideas		ILS_L4_U6_Listen
	Apply C		ILS_L4_U6_Speak_ApplyC
Pronunciation	Learn A		ILS_L4_U6_Pron_LearnA
	Apply A		ILS_L4_U6_Pron_ApplyA
	Apply B		ILS_L4_U6_Pron_ApplyB

UNIT 7

Listening	Listen		ILS_L4_U7_Listen
	Listen for Main Ideas		ILS_L4_U7_Listen
	Apply B		ILS_L4_U7_Note_ApplyB
	Apply C		ILS_L4_U7_Note_ApplyC
Speaking	Watch		ILS_L4_U7_Watch
	Listen for Main Ideas		ILS_L4_U7_Watch
	Apply B		ILS_L4_U7_Watch
Pronunciation	Learn A		ILS_L4_U7_Pron_LearnA
	Learn B		ILS_L4_U7_Pron_LearnB
	Apply A		ILS_L4_U7_Pron_ApplyA

UNIT 8

Listening	Watch		ILS_L4_U8_Watch
	Listen for Main Ideas		ILS_L4_U8_Watch
	Apply A		ILS_L4_U8_Note_ApplyA
Speaking	Listen		ILS_L4_U8_Listen
	Listen for Main Ideas		ILS_L4_U8_Listen
	Apply A		ILS_L4_U8_Listen
Pronunciation	Learn A		ILS_L4_U8_Pron_LearnA
	Apply A		ILS_L4_U8_Pron_ApplyA
	Apply B		ILS_L4_U8_Pron_ApplyB
	Apply C		ILS_L4_U8_Pron_ApplyC

UNIT 9

Listening	Listen		ILS_L4_U9_Listen
	Listen for Main Ideas		ILS_L4_U9_Listen
	Apply B		ILS_L4_U9_Listen_ApplyB
Speaking	Watch		ILS_L4_U9_Watch
	Listen for Main Ideas		ILS_L4_U9_Watch
	Apply B		ILS_L4_U9_Speak_ApplyB
Pronunciation	Learn A		ILS_L4_U9_Pron_LearnA
	Learn B		ILS_L4_U9_Pron_LearnA
	Apply A		ILS_L4_U9_Pron_ApplyA
	Apply B		ILS_L4_U9_Pron_ApplyB

UNIT 10

Listening	Listen		ILS_L4_U10_Listen1
	Listen for Main Ideas		ILS_L4_U10_Listen1
	Apply A		ILS_L4_U10_Note_ApplyA
Speaking	Listen		ILS_L4_U10_Listen2
	Listen for Main Ideas		ILS_L4_U10_Listen2
	Apply A		ILS_L4_U10_Listen2
Pronunciation	Learn A		ILS_L4_U10_Pron_LearnA
	Apply A		ILS_L4_U10_Pron_ApplyA
	Apply B		ILS_L4_U10_Pron_ApplyB
	Apply C		ILS_L4_U10_Pron_ApplyB

OXFORD
UNIVERSITY PRESS

198 Madison Avenue
New York, NY 10016 USA

Great Clarendon Street, Oxford, OX2 6DP, United Kingdom

Oxford University Press is a department of the University of Oxford.
It furthers the University's objective of excellence in research, scholarship,
and education by publishing worldwide. Oxford is a registered trade
mark of Oxford University Press in the UK and in certain other countries

First published in 2016

2020 2019 2018 2017 2016

10 9 8 7 6 5 4 3 2 1

Adult Content Director: Stephanie Karras
Publisher: Sharon Sargent
Managing Editor: Tracey Gibbins
Senior Development Editor: Anna Norris
Associate Editor: Rachael Xerri
Head of Digital, Design, and Production: Bridget O'Lavin
Executive Art and Design Manager: Maj-Britt Hagsted
Content Production Manager: Julie Armstrong
Design Project Manager: Mary Chandler
Image Manager: Trisha Masterson

ISBN: 978 0 19 471943 8

Printed in China

This book is printed on paper from certified and well-managed sources

ACKNOWLEDGEMENTS

*We would also like to thank the following for permission to reproduce the following
photographs:* **Cover**, Hervé de Gueltzl/Photononstop/Corbis; Tony Hallas/
Science Faction/Corbis; Marcel Jolibois/Photononstop/Corbis; Illustration
Works/Corbis; Apic/Contributor/Hulton Archive/Getty Images; Comstock/
Getty Images; Michele Westmorland/Getty Images; Eliks/shutterstock.
Interior, Alamy pp. 13 (making choices crossroads/MAC Photos), 40 (listening
to headphones/Blend Images), 80 (Ikaria island/Rolf Richardson), 100 (car
factory/TUN Gallery); Corbis UK Ltd. pp. 85 (good idea light bulb/TongRo
Images), 97 (robotic surgeon/laboratory), 104 (surgical robot/Digital Art); Getty
Images pp. 16 (child by bowl of marshmallows/doble.d), 44 (meeting/Klaus
Vedfelt), 47 (Voyager Golden Record/NASA/Handout), 112 (Inuit mother and
daughter/Veronique DURRUTY/Contributor); Oxford University Press pp. 28
(actors on set/fStop), 37 (violin with bow/Ocean), 68 (man with laptop/MJTH),
73 (gardening/EduardSV); Science Photo Library pp. 1 (Y shaped antibodies/
Animated Healthcare LTD), 4 (Felix Baumgartner jumping from capsule/
Ria Novosti); Shutterstock pp. 8 (giving vaccine/gorillaimages), 20 (people
running/Maridav), 25 (film clapboard/Aleksandr Bagri), 32 (urban garden/Arina
P Habich), 49 (3D neuron cell/Fedorov Oleksiy), 52 (brushing her teeth/AVAVA),
56 (students studying/Syda Productions), 61 (various dollars/lendy16), 64 (stack
of handmade hats/Tatiana Popova), 76 (mother and daughter with globe/Syda
Productions), 88 (laser cutter/Amnarj Tanongrattana), 92 (tractor in a field/
portumen), 109 (toy letter cubes/Ewa Studio), 116 (houses on the trees/Mirek
Nowaczyk).

Acknowledgements

We would like to acknowledge the following individuals for their input during the development of the series:

Salam Affouneh
Higher Colleges of Technology
Abu Dhabi, U.A.E.

Kristin Bouton
Intensive English Institute
Illinois, U.S.A.

Nicole H. Carrasquel
Center for Multilingual Multicultural Studies
Florida, U.S.A.

Elaine Cockerham
Higher College of Technology
Muscat, Oman

Danielle Dilkes
CultureWorks English as a Second Language Inc.
Ontario, Canada

Susan Donaldson
Tacoma Community College
Washington, U.S.A

Penelope Doyle
Higher Colleges of Technology
Dubai, U.A.E.

Edward Roland Gray
Yonsei University
Seoul, South Korea

Melanie Golbert
Higher Colleges of Technology
Abu Dhabi, U.A.E.

Elise Harbin
Alabama Language Institute
Alabama, U.S.A.

Bill Hodges
University of Guelph
Ontario, Canada

David Daniel Howard
National Chiayi University
Chiayi

Leander Hughes
Saitama Daigaku
Saitama, Japan

James Ishler
Higher Colleges of Technology
Fujairah, U.A.E.

John Iveson
Sheridan College
Ontario, Canada

Alan Lanes
Higher Colleges of Technology
Dubai, U.A.E.

Corinne Marshall
Fanshawe College
Ontario, Canada

Christine Matta
College of DuPage
Illinois, U.S.A.

Beth Montag
University at Kearney
Nebraska, U.S.A.

Kevin Mueller
Tokyo International University
Saitama, Japan

Tracy Anne Munteanu
Higher Colleges of Technology
Fujairah, U.A.E.

Eileen O'Brien
Khalifa University of Science, Technology, and Research
Sharjah, U.A.E.

Jangyo Parsons
Kookmin University
Seoul, South Korea

John P. Racine
Dokkyo Daigaku
Soka City, Japan

Scott Rousseau
American University of Sharjah
Sharjah, U.A.E.

Jane Ryther
American River College
California, U.S.A

Kate Tindle
Zayed University
Dubai, U.A.E.

Melody Traylor
Higher Colleges of Technology
Fujairah, U.A.E.

John Vogels
Higher Colleges of Technology
Dubai, U.A.E.

Kelly Wharton
Fanshawe College
Ontario, Canada

Contents

Unit 1 Your Body Fights Back   1

Content Area: Physiology

LISTENING AND SPEAKING SKILLS: Analogies and Metaphors;

Unit 2 Wait for It!   13

Content Area: Psychology

LISTENING AND SPEAKING SKILLS: Outlining Lecture Notes;

Unit 3 Film Know-How   25

Content Area: Film Studies

LISTENING AND SPEAKING SKILLS: Recording Definitions;

Unit 4 Sound Response   37

Content Area: Public Health

LISTENING AND SPEAKING SKILLS: Cause-and-Effect Relationships;

Unit 5 Changing Your Brain   49

Content Area: Neuroscience

LISTENING AND SPEAKING SKILLS: Listening for Signal Phrases;

The Inside Track to Academic Success

Student Books

For additional student resources, visit: www.insidelisteningandspeaking.com.

iTools for all levels

The *Inside Listening and Speaking* iTools component is for use with a projector or interactive whiteboard.

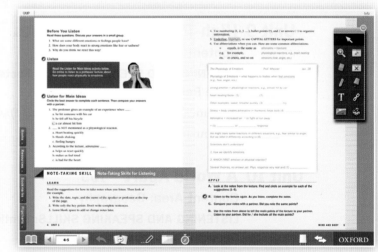

Resources for whole-class presentation

> **Book-on-screen** focuses class on teaching points and facilitates classroom management.

> **Audio and video** at point of use facilitates engaging, dynamic lessons.

Resources for assessment and preparation

> Customizable Unit, Mid-term, and Final Tests evaluate student progress.

> Complete Answer Keys are provided.

For additional instructor resources, visit:
www.oup.com/elt/teacher/insidelisteningandspeaking.

About *Inside Listening and Speaking*

Unit features

> **Explicit skills instruction** prepares students for academic listening

> **Authentic videos** from a variety of academic contexts engage and motivate students

> **Pronunciation instruction** ensures students are articulate, clear speakers

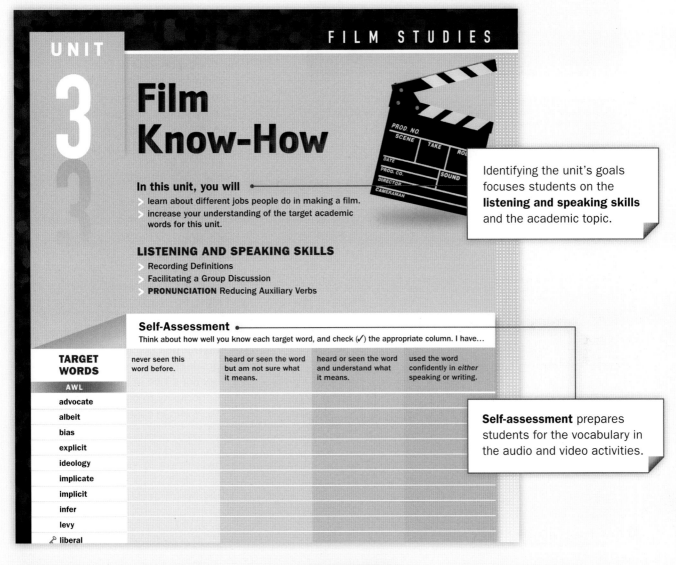

FILM STUDIES

UNIT

3

Film Know-How

In this unit, you will
> learn about different jobs people do in making a film.
> increase your understanding of the target academic words for this unit.

LISTENING AND SPEAKING SKILLS
> Recording Definitions
> Facilitating a Group Discussion
> **PRONUNCIATION** Reducing Auxiliary Verbs

Identifying the unit's goals focuses students on the **listening and speaking skills** and the academic topic.

Self-Assessment
Think about how well you know each target word, and check (✓) the appropriate column. I have…

TARGET WORDS	never seen this word before.	heard or seen the word but am not sure what it means.	heard or seen the word and understand what it means.	used the word confidently in *either* speaking or writing.
AWL				
advocate				
albeit				
bias				
explicit				
ideology				
implicate				
implicit				
infer				
levy				
🔑 liberal				

Self-assessment prepares students for the vocabulary in the audio and video activities.

The Academic Word List and the Oxford 3000

Based on a corpus of 4.3 million words, the **Academic Word List (AWL)** is the most principled and widely accepted list of academic words. Compiled by Averil Coxhead in 2000, it was informed by academic materials across the academic disciplines.

The **Oxford 3000™** have been carefully selected by a group of language experts and experienced teachers as the most important and useful words to learn in English. The Oxford 3000 are based on the American English section of the Oxford English Corpus.

Oxford 3000 and Academic Word List vocabulary is integrated throughout the unit and practiced in context through audio and video resources.

Explicit Skills Instruction

Before You Listen

Read these questions. Discuss your answers in a small group.

1. When you meet up with your friends, what do you often do for fun?
2. What kinds of films do you watch?
3. In filmmaking, what job interests you most? Explain your answer.

⊙ Listen

Read the Listen for Main Ideas activity below. Go online to listen to a podcast called *Behind the Scenes!* The host interviews several people working on the set of a new film.

⊙ Listen for Main Ideas

Mark each sentence as *T* (true) or *F* (false). Working with a partner, restate false sentences to make them correct.

___T___ 1. The film is an adventure story.
_____ 2. The director has more authority than the producer on everything.
_____ 3. A visual-effects artist has complete freedom during the design process.
_____ 4. A stunt person's job is not always easy.
_____ 5. Background actors are free to do what they want on the set.

NOTE-TAKING SKILL   Recording Definitions

LEARN

A definition tells you the meaning of a word or concept. Speakers often define important words and concepts for their audience. Listen for key phrases that tell you when the speaker is giving a definition.

> Filmmaking **is defined as** the process of creating motion pictures.
> Filmmaking **refers to** the production of motion pictures.
> A blockbuster film **is characterized by** great commercial success.
> A blockbuster film **signifies** great commercial success.

After the key phrase, a speaker will often give information that defines the word he / she is trying to describe.

Word being defined	Key phrase	Defining information
Filmmaking	is defined as	the process of creating motion pictures.

APPLY

⊙ **A.** Listen to the audio again. Match each job with the key phrase it is used with in the audio. Write brief notes about each job in the right column.

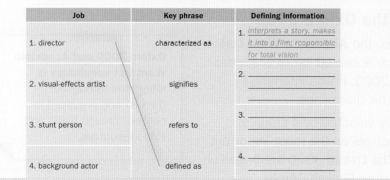

Job	Key phrase	Defining information
1. director	characterized as	1. *interprets a story, makes it into a film; responsible for total vision*
2. visual-effects artist	signifies	2. _____
3. stunt person	refers to	3. _____
4. background actor	defined as	4. _____

High-Interest Media Content

Before You Watch

Read the following questions. Discuss your answers in a small group.

1. If you were going to open a new business, what kind of business would you start?
2. What do you think is the hardest part of owning and operating a business?
3. What is the most successful industry in your country? Explain your answer.

Watch

Read the Listen for Main Ideas activity below. Go online to watch a podcast about how microcredit is helping people around the world create new lives for themselves.

Listen for Main Ideas

Mark each sentence as *T* (true) or *F* (false). Work with a partner. Restate false sentences to make them correct.

T 1. Microcredit is the process of providing small loans to people who normally would not be able to get a bank loan.

____ 2. The Grameen Bank has been in decline since it opened.

____ 3. The use of microcredit is growing in Africa.

____ 4. One problem with microcredit is that there is no incentive to repay the loan.

LISTENING SKILL   Inferences

LEARN

You make an inference when you decide that something is probably true based on the information that you have. Being able to make inferences is important because not all information is explicitly stated. When you make an inference, think about the speaker's opinion, attitude, and tone. Also, ask yourself what the speaker's purpose or area of interest is. Look at the example below.

"As a doctor, I say <u>regular health checks are no laughing matter</u>. I suggest going to see your local medical practitioner once a year. Regular check-ups can help prevent serious problems from developing."

The speaker is a doctor, promoting the importance of health checks. Based on this information, we can reasonably infer that the statement "regular health checks are no laughing matter" means that getting a regular check-up is an important thing to do.

Audio and video including lectures, professional presentations, classroom discussions, and student presentations expose students to a **variety of academic contexts**.

High-interest, original academic video and authentic BBC content motivate students.

Pronunciation Instruction

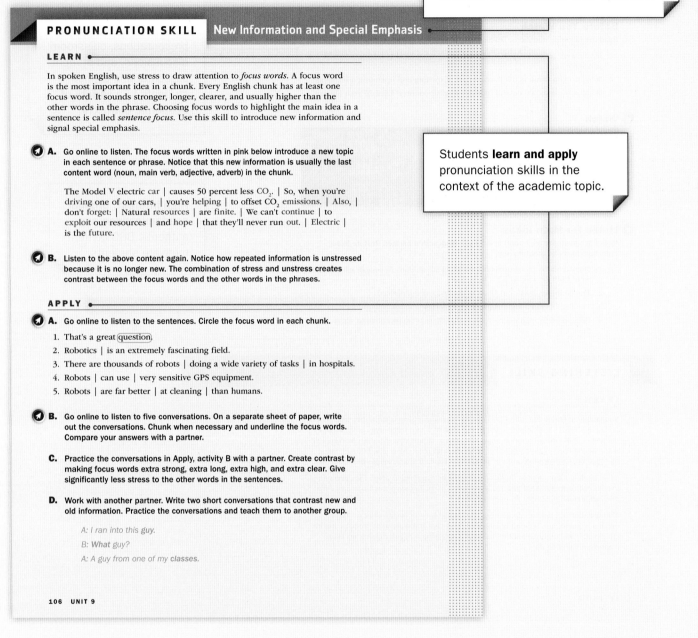

PRONUNCIATION SKILL   New Information and Special Emphasis

LEARN

In spoken English, use stress to draw attention to *focus words*. A focus word is the most important idea in a chunk. Every English chunk has at least one focus word. It sounds stronger, longer, clearer, and usually higher than the other words in the phrase. Choosing focus words to highlight the main idea in a sentence is called *sentence focus*. Use this skill to introduce new information and signal special emphasis.

A. Go online to listen. The focus words written in pink below introduce a new topic in each sentence or phrase. Notice that this new information is usually the last content word (noun, main verb, adjective, adverb) in the chunk.

The Model V electric car | causes 50 percent less CO_2. | So, when you're driving one of our cars, | you're helping | to offset CO_2 emissions. | Also, | don't forget: | Natural resources | are finite. | We can't continue | to exploit our resources | and hope | that they'll never run out. | Electric | is the future.

B. Listen to the above content again. Notice how repeated information is unstressed because it is no longer new. The combination of stress and unstress creates contrast between the focus words and the other words in the phrases.

APPLY

A. Go online to listen to the sentences. Circle the focus word in each chunk.

1. That's a great question.
2. Robotics | is an extremely fascinating field.
3. There are thousands of robots | doing a wide variety of tasks | in hospitals.
4. Robots | can use | very sensitive GPS equipment.
5. Robots | are far better | at cleaning | than humans.

B. Go online to listen to five conversations. On a separate sheet of paper, write out the conversations. Chunk when necessary and underline the focus words. Compare your answers with a partner.

C. Practice the conversations in Apply, activity B with a partner. Create contrast by making focus words extra strong, extra long, extra high, and extra clear. Give significantly less stress to the other words in the sentences.

D. Work with another partner. Write two short conversations that contrast new and old information. Practice the conversations and teach them to another group.

A: I ran into this **guy**.

B: **What** guy?

A: A guy from one of my **classes**.

106   UNIT 9

UNIT 1

Your Body Fights Back

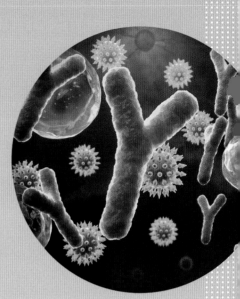

In this unit, you will

> learn about how the body reacts under extreme conditions.

> increase your understanding of the target academic words for this unit.

LISTENING AND SPEAKING SKILLS

> Analogies and Metaphors

> Introducing a Presentation

> **PRONUNCIATION** Rhythm

Self-Assessment

Think about how well you know each target word, and check (✓) the appropriate column. I have…

TARGET WORDS	never seen this word before.	heard or seen the word but am not sure what it means.	heard or seen the word and understand what it means.	used the word confidently in *either* speaking or writing.
AWL				
analogy				
🔑 considerable				
convene				
dispose				
enforce				
🔑 ensure				
🔑 expose				
induce				
infrastructure				
legislate				
migrate				
practitioner				
transmit				
trigger				

🔑 Oxford 3000™ keywords

Vocabulary Activities

Word Form Chart			
Noun	**Verb**	**Adjective**	**Adverb**
_____	_____	considerable	considerably
convention	convene	conventional unconventional	conventionally
_____	ensure	_____	_____
exposure	expose	exposed	_____
trigger	trigger	_____	_____

A. Complete the paragraph below with the target words from the Word Form Chart. Use the correct form and tense of each word.

In recent years, space tourism has gained ___considerable___ attention, despite
      (1. great in amount)

the expense. The world's first space tourist, American Dennis Tito, paid

20 million dollars for his _____ trip to space. Additionally, the
                            (2. uncommon)

opportunity for profit has _____ the creation of many new space
                          (3. made happen)

tourism companies. Many people, seeking _____ to weightlessness
                                       (4. having an experience)

in space, have signed up for future trips. Currently, these space tourism

companies are working hard to _____ safe, low-cost trips to space
                             (5. make certain)

are available in the future.

B. Some words have multiple meanings. For the target words below, match the dictionary definitions on the left with the example sentences on the right.

expose

Definitions

__c__ 1. to show the truth about
       somebody or something

____ 2. to leave something uncovered
       or unprotected

____ 3. to provide an experience

Example Sentences

a. Fruit juice can go bad if it is exposed
   to the sun.

b. Some parents think it's important to
   expose their children to books and
   music at a young age.

c. The investigation exposed problems
   with company management.

Definitions

____ 1. a large meeting of the members of a profession or political party

____ 2. an official agreement between countries or leaders

____ 3. a traditional method or style in literature or the arts

Example Sentences

a. The United Nations Convention on the Rights of Children was signed in 1989.

b. Several officials attended the convention on climate change.

c. The conventions used in academic writing are different from those used for spoken English.

Transmit means "to send an electronic signal."

The radio station **transmits** from a large tower.

Transmit also means "to pass from one person or thing to another."

Malaria is a disease that is **transmitted** by mosquitoes.

 CORPUS

C. Complete the chart. Share your answers with a partner.

Things transmitted by electronic signals	Things transmitted from one person to another
1. _a radio broadcast_	1. _a disease_
2. _____	2. _____
3. _____	3. _____

Analogy means "a comparison of one thing with another thing that has similar features." The adjective *analogous* means "similar in some way to another thing or situation and therefore able to be compared with it." *Analogous* is often used with the preposition *to.*

The new policy is **analogous to** the old policy. Both fail to solve our problems.

 CORPUS

D. Choose the phrase on the right that best completes each sentence on the left.

_c_ 1. The conditions on the planet of Mars are analogous

____ 2. With its state-of-the-art facilities, the new home for elderly people is analogous

____ 3. Snow helps keep soil warmer in winter, so it is analogous

a. to a five-star hotel.

b. to a blanket.

c. to those found in deserts on Earth.

About the Topic

Altitude is height above sea or ground level. As you go up in altitude, air pressure decreases. This change has an effect on our bodies.

Before You Listen

Read these questions. Discuss your answers in a small group.

1. Would you ever go skydiving? Why or why not?
2. What are the most extreme temperature or weather conditions you have experienced?
3. Do you think space tourism will become a common way to travel in the future?

Listen

Read the Listen for Main Ideas activity below. Go online to listen to a news report on the world's first space jump. The report discusses how scientists studied Felix Baumgartner's body when he jumped from 24 miles above Earth's surface.

Listen for Main Ideas

Mark each sentence as *T* (true) or *F* (false). Work with a partner. Restate false sentences to make them correct.

_F_ 1. Felix Baumgartner jumped from below where planes normally fly.

He jumped from above where planes fly.

____ 2. It took a long time to prepare for Baumgartner's jump.

____ 3. Air pressure does not affect the body.

____ 4. Baumgartner's jump gave scientists new information about the human body.

LISTENING SKILL   Analogies and Metaphors

LEARN

When you use figurative language, like *analogies* and *metaphors*, you use words or phrases in a way that creates a mental picture for the listener.

An analogy compares two different things to show that they have similar characteristics. The words and phrases *as*, *like*, and *the same as* are often used in analogies. Speakers use analogies to help their listeners visualize, understand, remember, and form conclusions about what is being said.

Life is like taking a journey around the world. You experience new things every day. With these new experiences, your understanding and knowledge increase, and you become better able to prepare for and deal with challenges.

A metaphor shows how two things have the same characteristics. A metaphor can create a strong image for the listener. A metaphor does <u>not</u> use the words and phrases *as, like,* or *the same as.*

My throat is on fire.   *Time is a thief.*

APPLY

A. Write *A* if the sentence contains an analogy or *M* if it contains a metaphor.

_M_ 1. Waves of emails came after she announced her retirement.

___ 2. Some people think attending university is the same as a long vacation and that the real work begins after graduation. This is just not true.

___ 3. Being in that class was like being on a sinking ship.

___ 4. He was lost in a sea of people.

B. Go online to listen to part of the audio. Fill in the blanks below. After listening, mark the statements as either *M* (metaphor) or *A* (analogy) in the right column.

1. Baumgartner's suit worked _much like an airplane_ ... by controlling airflow and air pressure and providing protection from the cold.	_A_
2. In other words, he _____, moving faster than the speed of sound.	___
3. Doctors and scientists placed equipment on Baumgartner _____ _____ being sent on a long mission into space.	___
4. As Baumgartner landed, the team that had designed his suit _____ _____, cheering and hugging one another.	___
5. His suit worked _____, protecting his body and helping him become the first human being to move faster than the speed of sound with just his body.	___
6. Having stood _____ and survived, Baumgartner has given scientists new information about how the body reacts under extreme conditions.	___

C. Work in a small group to create an analogy using each pair below. Discuss.

1. exercising / watering a garden

   Exercising is like watering a garden. If you do it every day, you (like your plants) will be healthy and strong.

2. ants / human beings

3. starting a new job / starting a journey

D. Work in a small group to create a metaphor using each pair below. Discuss.

1. basketball / medicine

   Basketball was her medicine. It helped relieve her stress.

2. the lecture / a gift

3. the exam / insane

Word Form Chart		
Noun	**Verb**	**Adjective**
disposal	dispose	disposable
enforcement	enforce	_____
induction	induce	_____
legislation legislature	legislate	legislative
practitioner	_____	_____

A. Complete the paragraph below with the target words from the Word Form Chart. Use the correct form and tense of each word.

Sometimes, when lawmakers create new health care ___*legislation*___, they
(1. rulings)

have difficulty understanding complex medical issues. Last year, to avoid

this problem, the _____ asked for advice from a group of medical
(2. lawmaking part of government)

_____ in writing a new health care law, which required that all
(3. professionals)

children over the age of seven receive vaccinations against certain diseases.

However, _____ the new law proved difficult. In some cities, the
(4. making sure people follow)

law _____ protest and anger because of the high fees charged
(5. caused something to happen)

for the vaccinations. As a result, some lawmakers are considering

_____ of the new requirement while searching for ways to lower
(6. getting rid)

the cost of vaccinations.

B. Match the definitions on the left with the example sentences on the right.

dispose of

Definitions

_c_ 1. to deal with a problem successfully

____ 2. to get rid of something

____ 3. to defeat one's opponent

Example Sentences

a. It only took the new chess champion 20 minutes to dispose of the previous one.

b. I'm not sure how to dispose of paint.

c. The firm managed to dispose of the problem by creating a new rule.

A *practitioner* is "a person who works in a profession, especially medicine or law."

*Jonas and Miguel are health care **practitioners**; one is a doctor, the other a nurse.*

Practitioner also means "a person who regularly does a particular activity, especially one that requires skill."

*The students are **practitioners** of the art of drama.*

C. Choose the phrase on the right that best completes each sentence on the left.

_a_ 1. The new tax office helps local nutrition practitioners

2. The Lake District became a center for arts and crafts pratcitioners,

3. Hiro became a nurse practitioner, and now he

a. accurately report their income each year.

b. can treat medical problems without the supervision of a doctor.

c. allowing people to develop many traditional skills plus a few new ones.

D. *Infrastructure* is "the basic systems and services that are necessary for a country or an organization to run smoothly, for example, buildings, transportation, and water and power supplies." Work with a partner. Note and discuss three important components of the infrastructure of the city you live in.

1. _the bus system_ .

2. _____ .

3. _____ .

Migrate means "to move from one part of the world to another according to the season." In this sense, it usually refers to animals, especially some birds.

*These birds **migrate** from the Arctic to Mexico for the winter.*

In technical language, *migrate* also means "to move from one place to another."

*The virus will **migrate** to different parts of the body.*

E. How or why do the following things migrate? Discuss your ideas with a partner.

1. Birds: to find food, _____ , _____

2. Viruses: by direct contact, _____ , _____

About the Topic

The flu, or influenza, is a type of virus that causes disease. If a person has immunity to a virus, it means the virus does not affect the person's body. A vaccination is a substance that is put into the blood in order to give a person immunity to a disease.

Before You Listen

Read these questions. Discuss your answers in a small group.

1. What are some things you do to avoid viruses and other illnesses?

2. Do you think laws should require people to get vaccinated for the flu? Explain your answer.

3. What kinds of foods do you eat to give you energy or to fight an illness?

Listen

Read the Listen for Main Ideas activity below. Go online to listen to a doctor discuss how to prevent the flu. She also talks about how vaccinations work.

Listen for Main Ideas

Listen to the audio. Circle the letter of the answer that correctly completes each sentence.

1. The flu virus ____.
   - a. moves quickly from person to person
   - c. usually stays in one place
   - b. moves slowly from person to person

2. Antibodies ____.
   - a. hurt your body
   - c. help your body fight the flu
   - b. support the flu

3. Herd immunity means that most people in a population ____.
   - a. are not affected by a certain disease
   - c. are not affected by antibodies
   - b. can easily get a certain illness

4. Vaccinations ____.
   - a. stop antibodies
   - c. cause illness
   - b. create herd immunity

5. Vaccinations for the students ____.
   - a. are expensive
   - c. are free
   - b. take time to get

PRESENTATION SKILL | Introducing a Presentation

LEARN

A formal presentation consists of an introduction, body, and conclusion. A good introduction to your presentation grabs the attention of the audience and helps them gain a clear understanding of what you are presenting. The following suggestions can help create a good introduction to a presentation.

1. Start with a brief greeting and tell your audience what your topic is.	Good afternoon. I'm going to talk about … I'm Judith Chen. I'm here to discuss …
2. Use an interesting hook such as an attention-grabbing question, statistic, photo, or quote.	Do you know how many … ? There are one million people who … "The art of medicine consists of amusing the patient." —Voltaire
3. Briefly explain the relevance or importance of your presentation topic.	This topic is important because … This research can help us … We have much to learn about …
4. Give the audience an outline of your presentation.	First, I'm going to show you … Then, I'm going to give you examples of … After that, we'll look at … Finally, I will take questions.

APPLY

A. Listen to the first part of the presentation. As you listen, write the expressions the presenter uses while introducing her presentation.

Step 1	_Good afternoon._ It is very nice to be here today. My name is Dr. Linda Carrol, and I'm from the school health clinic. _____ how we can prevent the flu virus, also known as influenza.
Step 2	Let me ask you this: _____ have had the flu virus?
Step 3	Now, the flu virus migrates quickly from one person to the next, and it can keep you in bed for days. So, _____ how we can prevent the flu.
Step 4	So, first, _____ what the flu is. Then, _____ you how our bodies fight it. Finally, _____ how we can prevent the flu.

B. Work in a group of three or four. Develop an introduction for a presentation on one of the following topics:

1. how to fight an illness
2. how to survive your first year of college or first year working for a company
3. how to learn new vocabulary in English

Step 1	
Step 2	
Step 3	
Step 4	

LEARN

Rhythm is a pattern of sound, and every language has its own particular rhythm. English rhythm has strong and weak sounds. Strong, important syllables come at regular intervals, and you say them fully and completely. Weak, unimportant syllables are shortened and squeezed in between the strong sounds.

Strong sounds are usually nouns, adjectives, adverbs, and main verbs. Weak words are usually articles, pronouns, prepositions, and auxiliary verbs.

A. Go online to listen to the rhythm. Notice that it takes the same amount of time to say the words in each box.

O N E	T W O	T H R E E	F O U R
ONE and	**TWO** and	**THREE** and	**FOUR** and
ONE and a	**TWO** and a	**THREE** and a	**FOUR** and a
ONE-ey and a	**TWO**-ey and a	**THREE**-ey and a	**FOUR**-ey and a

B. Listen to and repeat the words in Learn, activity A. Say all of the words. Keep the rhythm.

C. Go online to listen to the sentences in the chart below. Notice how the weak words are shortened in order to maintain the rhythm.

	1	2		3
	COWS		EAT	GRASS.
The	COWS	can	EAT	the GRASS.
The	COWS	are	EATing	some GRASS.
His	COWS	have	EATen	their GRASS.
Some	COWS	will be	EATing	the GRASS.
Their	COWS	might have	EATen	the GRASS.
The	COWS	are going to be	EATing	the GRASS.
The	COWS	should not have been EATing		our GRASS.

APPLY

A. Listen to and repeat the sentences in Learn, activity C with the speaker. Match the rhythm. Tap out the beat, so you can really hear it.

B. Go online to listen to the content of the chart on page 11. The words and sentences in each column have the same stress pattern and rhythm. Repeat the words and sentences with a partner.

	●●	•●	●•••	•●••	•●•••
Word	migrate	induce	infrastructure	analogy	considerable
Sentence	Do it!	Here's why.	Wait a minute!	They've triggered it.	I'm counting on you!

C. Write a short dialogue. Then share it with a partner. Pay careful attention to the rhythm of your dialogues.

A: The bus is leaving. I have to run.   *B: Hey! Wait a minute!*

End of Unit Task

In this unit, you learned how to listen for analogies and metaphors, and how to give an introduction to a presentation. Watch a short video on the flu. Then develop an introduction to a presentation with a partner.

A. Go online to watch a video about how the body fights the flu. Take notes on the metaphors that the speaker uses.

1. Inside him, his body is about to engage in _____*all-out war*_____ with one of the most infectious viruses on the planet.

2. Flu viruses start _____ the tissue at the back of your throat.

3. Meanwhile, _____ of phagocytes floods the infection site. They have come to _____ their enemies.

4. It's a sign _____ inside him is heating up.

5. His body has launched a second _____.

B. Work with a partner. Considering ideas from the video, create an analogy about the flu. Refer to page 4 for a description of analogies. Include one or two statements that explain and support your analogy.

When your body fights the flu, the process is like two teams at a sporting event. They both go against each other, with each team trying to score more points than the other.

C. Work with a partner to develop an introduction for a presentation on how the body fights the flu. Use the steps for introducing a presentation, on page 9.

Step 1: _____

Step 2: _____

Step 3: _____

Step 4: _____

D. Divide the parts of the presentation between you and your partner and practice giving your presentation. After practicing, revise your presentation.

E. Take turns sharing your presentation with another group.

F. Use the following chart to give feedback on the presentation you heard. For each part of the introduction, share your feedback with the other group.

Start with a brief greeting, telling your audience what your topic is.	a. clear and easy to understand b. somewhat clear and easy to understand c. unclear and difficult to understand
Use an interesting analogy or metaphor as a hook for your presentation.	a. clear and interesting b. somewhat clear and interesting c. unclear and uninteresting
Briefly explain the relevance or importance of your presentation topic.	a. clear and easy to understand b. somewhat clear and easy to understand c. unclear and difficult to understand
Give the audience an outline of your presentation.	a. clear and easy to understand b. somewhat clear and easy to understand c. unclear and difficult to understand

G. Discuss your presentations as a class.

1. What did you do well?

2. What would you do differently?

3. What is the hardest part of creating an introduction for a presentation?

Self-Assessment		
Yes	**No**	
☐	☐	I learned to listen for metaphors and analogies.
☐	☐	I gave an introduction to a presentation.
☐	☐	I was able to provide feedback on the introduction to a presentation.
☐	☐	I paid attention to rhythm when speaking, using strong and weak sounds.
☐	☐	I can correctly use the target vocabulary words from the unit.

Discussion Questions

With a partner or in a small group, discuss the following questions.

1. Before doing physical activity, what do you do to prepare your body?

2. What is the most challenging physical activity or training you have ever done?

3. Do you think an athlete's success is based more on natural ability or on hard work and training?

UNIT 2

Wait for It!

In this unit, you will
> learn about how the mind matures as we get older.
> increase your understanding of the target academic words for this unit.

LISTENING AND SPEAKING SKILLS
> Outlining Lecture Notes
> Stating, Rephrasing, and Illustrating
> **PRONUNCIATION** Reducing Function Words

Self-Assessment
Think about how well you know each target word, and check (✓) the appropriate column. I have...

TARGET WORDS	never seen this word before.	heard or seen the word but am not sure what it means.	heard or seen the word and understand what it means.	used the word confidently in *either* speaking or writing.
AWL				
🔑 accompany				
🔑 circumstance				
consequent				
discrete				
distinct				
erode				
implement				
incentive				
inhibit				
🔑 justify				
paradigm				
prime				
🔑 sufficient				
undertake				

🔑 Oxford 3000™ keywords

Vocabulary Activities

Word Form Chart			
Noun	**Verb**	**Adjective**	**Adverb**
consequence	_____	consequent	consequently
distinction	_____	distinct distinctive	distinctly
incentive	_____	_____	_____
inhibition	inhibit	inhibited	_____
sufficiency	_____	sufficient	sufficiently

A. Complete the paragraph below with the target words from the Word Form Chart. Use the correct form and tense of each word.

Many psychologists consider the years between the ages of 18 and 29 to be

a(n) ___*distinct*___ stage of an adult's life. During this time, a person's brain
(1. clearly different)

is still maturing. One part of the brain, called the *frontal lobe*, _____
(2. prevents from happening)

the need for immediate gratification. *Gratification* means "feeling pleasure

when your desires are satisfied." Therefore, the frontal lobe is important

because it considers the _____ of actions as well as the possibility
(3. results)

of future _____ for delaying gratification. However, from 18 to 29
(4. things that encourage you to do something)

years of age, the frontal lobe is not yet completely mature. _____,
(5. as a result)

some psychologists believe that people should delay major life decisions

related to marriage or a career until the brain has _____ time to
(6. enough)

develop.

Erode means "to gradually destroy the surface of something" by rain, wind,
or water.

> Deforestation may cause the soil to **erode**, which can decrease a farmer's ability
> to grow crops.

Erode also means "to gradually destroy something or make it weaker over a
period of time," especially ideas, values, or feelings.

> The panel of professors debated whether or not globalization has **eroded**
> traditional customs in some parts of the world.

CORPUS

B. Work with a partner. Discuss different things that can erode.

    Surfaces: soil, sand dunes, _____, _____, _____

    Ideas, Values, Feelings: privacy, confidence, _____, _____,

    _____

Distinct describes something that is "clearly heard, seen, or felt."

    (a) He heard the **distinct** sound of footsteps in the other room.

Distinct also means "clearly different or of a different kind."

    (b) Although Axel and Manny are twins, each boy has a **distinct** personality.

CORPUS

C. Write *a* or *b* to show which usage of *distinct* or *indistinct* is being used in each sentence.

  _b_ 1. Her paintings had a distinct look. All of the other paintings were fairly similar to one another.

  ___ 2. There are distinct differences between the two schools. For instance, the first school is a technical high school.

  ___ 3. She has a distinct voice. We can hear her even when it is noisy.

  ___ 4. While camping, he heard an indistinct sound in the forest.

  ___ 5. It was hard to find the right building. Every building in the neighborhood had the same indistinct look.

D. *Implement* means "to make something that has been officially decided start to happen or be used." Complete each sentence with a word from the box. More than one answer is possible for some items. Review your answers with a partner.

plan	policy	recommendation	strategy	system

1. The lawyer implemented his ___*strategy*___ during the trial. It was a success.

2. The government implemented the new health care _____ last year.

3. The university has implemented a new online _____ for selecting classes.

4. They implemented the _____ that their supervisor had suggested.

E. *Sufficient* means "enough for a particular purpose." Circle the word or phrase in parentheses that makes each sentence true for you. Discuss your answers with a partner.

1. The place where I live has a(n) (*sufficient / insufficient*) number of restaurants, museums, and parks.

2. In my country, the amount of money spent by the government on education is (*sufficient / insufficient*).

3. I spend a(n) (*sufficient / insufficient*) amount of time studying for this class.

About the Topic

The frontal lobe is a part of the brain that considers the results of an action. The frontal lobe develops as we get older. As a result, adults are normally better than children at resisting short-term desires and making long-term decisions.

Before You Watch

Read these questions. Discuss your answers in a small group.

1. What incentives motivated you to study when you were in high school?

2. When you make a decision, which is more important to you: short-term gratification or long-term incentives?

3. Psychology is often used to help people. What are some other ways that psychology is used?

Watch

Read the Listen for Main Ideas activity below. Go online to watch a video about the Stanford Marshmallow Experiment. The experiment shows that success in life may be related to your ability to avoid certain actions such as eating sweets.

Listen for Main Ideas

Work with a partner to answer the following questions.

1. What incentive was offered to the children in the Stanford University Marshmallow Experiment?

   They could eat one piece of a treat now or wait for 15 minutes and get three pieces.

2. What was different about the children who were able to wait?

3. What did the brain scans show?

4. What did the BBC and Open University Experiment show?

NOTE-TAKING SKILL   Outlining Lecture Notes

LEARN

Outlining is one way to take notes. Notice how the video on the Stanford University Marshmallow Experiment is outlined on page 17. There are five main sections (A–E). Under each main section, there is also space to record supporting information and key words (1, 2, 3, …). When you outline, do not write full sentences. Just write the main ideas.

Lecture Topic: Incentives and Decision-Making

I. The Stanford Marshmallow Experiment
  A. Done by Mischel in 1970s
    1. gave insight → how people react to incentives
    2. one treat now / _____

  B. During Experiment
    1. about 1/2 kids = _____
    2. other kids = _____

  C. _____
    1. younger children, _____ *frontal lobe*
    2. younger children harder to _____

  D. Other results: as adults ...
    1. individuals who waited = _____
    2. individuals who didn't wait = _____
    3. Later, Mischel found differences in _____

  E. Other studies
    _____

APPLY

A. Watch the first part of the lecture again and fill in the outline above.

B. Compare your outline with a partner. Add any important information that you missed.

C. Working with your partner, take turns summarizing the lecture in your own words by using your outlines.

D. Watch the BBC and Open University video again. Write an outline for the video and compare outlines with a different partner.

II. BBC + Open University Experiment
  A. Children = immature frontal lobes
     resisting temptation difficult

  B. _____
    1. _____
    2. _____

  C. _____
    1. _____
    2. _____

Vocabulary Activities

A. Cross out the word or phrase in parentheses that has a different meaning from the others. Use a dictionary to help you understand new words.

1. Online courses represent a new (*standard* / ~~*request*~~ / *paradigm* / *model*) in education.

2. The (*skill* / *job* / *undertaking* / *task*) required the team to develop a new strategy in just two days.

3. There is no (*enthusiasm* / *justification* / *defense* / *explanation*) for not having your homework completed on time. You had two weeks to complete it.

4. (*In certain circumstances* / *For certain incomes* / *In certain situations* / *Under certain conditions*), a junior member of the team may lead a project.

5. There is a (*discrete* / *unknown* / *distinct* / *clear*) difference between psychology and sociology.

6. The athlete is (*at the end of* / *in the prime of* / *at a highpoint in* / *at the best part of*) his career and performing very well.

7. Mr. Kauffman could not (*think of a reason for* / *justify* / *rationalize* / *assist in*) spending $40 for a T-shirt.

Accompany means "to go somewhere with someone" or "to happen or appear with something else."

> *Markus normally **accompanies** the manager on business trips.*

> *The increase in unemployment **accompanied** the decline in the stock market.*

Accompany is often used in the passive voice.

> *At the swimming pool, children must **be accompanied** by their parents.*

> *High winds **are** often **accompanied** by lower temperatures.*

CORPUS

B. To practice correctly using the word *accompany*, choose the phrase on the right that best completes each sentence on the left.

<u>d</u> 1. Lightning is often accompanied   a. my friend on his fishing trips.

___ 2. A photo and a transcript must accompany   b. by text that provided explanations.

___ 3. I rarely accompany   c. all applications.

___ 4. Visitors must be accompanied   d. by thunder.

___ 5. The images were accompanied   e. by guides at all times.

C. *Undertake* means "to make yourself responsible for something and start doing it." Fill in the chart below and discuss the tasks / projects with a partner.

a task / project that you recently undertook	
a task / project that you plan to undertake sometime this year	
a task / project that a company, government, or other organization has recently undertaken	

D. Write the letter of the definition on the line before each sentence that best matches the meaning of *prime* as used in that sentence.

a. most likely to be chosen for something	b. main or most important	c. of the best quality

_c_ 1. The downtown area is prime real estate. The value of land there is very high and the area is incredibly beautiful.

___ 2. The seat that I had was a prime location for watching the performance, which I really enjoyed.

___ 3. My prime interest is in developmental psychology.

___ 4. The local market has a prime selection of fruits and vegetables.

___ 5. Maria is a prime candidate for the position of mayor.

___ 6. Aziz was a prime target for the study because of his age.

___ 7. His prime concern was maintaining the safety of his home.

E. A *paradigm shift* is "a great and important change in the way something is done or thought about." List technological inventions that have led to a paradigm shift. Discuss your answers with a partner.

1. *the smartphone*

2. *the television*

3. _____

4. _____

5. _____

6. _____

About the Topic

Self-improvement refers to improving oneself through one's own efforts and abilities. Self-improvement might include efforts to expand one's career success, personal finance, public speaking, health, or other personal interests. In 2013, the self-improvement industry was worth several billion dollars worldwide.

Before You Listen

Read these questions. Discuss your answers in a small group.

1. What major goals have you set for yourself this year?

2. What is the best way for a person to accomplish his / her goals?

3. What kinds of self-improvement programs or tasks have you considered trying?

⊘ Listen

Read the Listen for Main Ideas activity below. Go online to listen to an interview with a motivational speaker and author. He describes a four-step plan for achieving self-improvement goals.

⊘ Listen for Main Ideas

Read the questions about the presentation. Work with a partner to choose the best answer to complete each sentence.

1. According to the interview, goals are often difficult to accomplish because they ____.

    a. are expensive and time-consuming ⓒ require hard work

    b. do not keep a person's interest

2. The first step in Dr. Fogg's "Tiny Habits" program focuses on ____.

    a. having long-term goals   c. building confidence slowly

    b. making small changes

3. Kris Ryan suggests making activities easier to do so that ____.

    a. you have enough time   c. you don't feel bad about failure

    b. you have no reason not to do them

4. Giving yourself credit and praise for your accomplishments ____.

    a. can help you move forward   c. is not necessary but useful

    b. is easy for everyone

PRESENTATION SKILL   Stating, Rephrasing, and Illustrating

LEARN

When you state a main point or idea, rephrasing (or saying it again in different words) can help you to clarify your idea. Then you can illustrate the idea by using a specific example. This process gives the listener a better opportunity to understand and process what you have said.

Step 1 – State: State the main point or idea.

To accomplish your goals, you should try to set short-term objectives.

Step 2 – Rephrase: Restate the main point, or say it in a different way. Use key phrases to let your audience know you are rephrasing.

To put it differently, take smaller steps toward achieving your goals.
In other words, take smaller steps toward achieving your goals.
Another way to say this is that you should take smaller steps.
What I mean by that is that you should take smaller steps.

Step 3 – Illustrate: Illustrate the idea with an example.

For instance, plan just your afternoon instead of the whole month.
To give you a specific example, plan just your afternoon instead of the whole month.

APPLY

A. Listen to part of the audio again. Fill in the chart below.

State	Rephrase	Illustrate
Self-improvement means undertaking a new task or project to achieve a goal.	_____, the goal is accompanied by physical or mental work.	So, _____, you want to get in better shape but that requires exercise / changing how or what you eat.
OK. Well, tiny step number one is _____.	_____ is: Don't set huge, long-term goals. Instead, try for small successes.	_____, rather than deciding to lose 18 pounds in a month, commit to eating less for dinner and doing exercise tomorrow before work.
Tiny step number two: make new tasks easier to do	_____ is plan properly, so you have no justification for *not* doing what you wanted to do.	_____ that you go running every morning, but you don't feel very motivated at 7 a.m.

B. Look at the information about "tiny step" three. Working with a partner, discuss the correct order of the sentences.

- To put it differently, don't place all of your emphasis on the old, unwanted habits.

- So, to give you a specific example, instead of letting yourself get stressed about how you watch too much TV, change the circumstances that normally lead you to watch TV by planning a productive, fun activity for yourself.

- The third tiny step is to focus on creating new, positive behaviors.

C. Work with partner. Choose two of the four "tiny steps." Next, state, rephrase, and illustrate each step in your own words. Then present your explanation of the two "tiny steps" to another group.

LEARN

Function words include articles, auxiliary verbs, pronouns, prepositions, and short conjunctions. These are "grammar words" that carry relatively little information in a sentence. Because function words are considered "less important," they usually contain the short, quiet schwa sound /ə/, which makes them difficult to hear.

 A. Look at the chart and go online to listen to the pronunciation. Notice how function words and the main verbs *be* and *have* are reduced.

Articles / Determiners	a → ə	an → ən	the → thə	some → səm	
Prepositions	for → fər	from → frəm	in → ən	to → tə / də	h̷e
Pronouns	you → yə	your → yər	that → thət	it → ət	h̷is
Short conjunctions	and → ən	or → ər	but → bət	that → thət	h̷er →
"Be" (main verb)	is → əz	are → ər	was → wəz	were → wər	h̷im
"Have" (main verb)	has → əz	have → /əv/	had → /əd/		them

 B. Look at the chart and go online to listen to the reductions. Unstressed function words often sound the same.

1	2	3	4	5	6	7	8	9
/ə/	/əm/	/ən/	/ər/	/ət/	/əv/	/əz/	/s/	/z/
a	am	an	or	it	of	is	is	is
of	him	in	are	at	have	as		
	them	and	her			his		
						has		

APPLY

 A. Go online to listen to the phrases below. Practice common collocations with the reduced function words *and*, *or*, and *of*. What other phrases do you know? Share them with a partner.

and	or	of
1. brothers and sisters	4. Soup or salad?	7. out of work
2. Ladies and Gentlemen!	5. Debit or credit?	8. Piece of cake!
3. Cream and sugar?	6. For here or to go?	9. the cost of living

B. Pair the adjectives and animals to make idioms. Make sentences. Practice the sentences with a partner. Listen for the reduced function words.

Adjectives: blind, easy, hungry, quiet, stubborn, wise

Nouns: a bear, a mule, an owl, a bat, a mouse, pie

blind as a bat — Without my glasses, I'm as blind as a bat.

C. Listen to ten sentences with reduced function words. Write the sentences using full forms of the words. Then practice saying the sentences to a partner.

6 words / Whatser dayda birth? → What is her date of birth?

End of Unit Task

In this unit, you learned how to outline lecture notes. You also learned how to help your audience understand your presentations by stating, rephrasing, and illustrating mains ideas. Practice both of these skills by planning a short presentation.

A. Choose one of the following topics to present.

- Present three interesting aspects of either your culture or another culture that you are familiar with.
- Present three keys to success at college or in a career.
- Present three tips for traveling on a small budget.

B. Develop your presentation. For parts A, B, and C in the outline below, state, rephrase, and illustrate each main point.

Title

I. (Introduction)

II. (Body)

   A.

   B.

   C.

III. (Conclusion)

C. Work with a partner. Listen to each other's presentations. As you listen, outline your partner's presentation.

Title

I.

II.

   A.

   B.

   C.

III.

D. After outlining your partner's presentation, choose one of your partner's main points and state, rephrase, and illustrate it in your own words.

Yes	No	Self-Assessment
☐	☐	I learned to outline lecture notes.
☐	☐	I was able to state, rephrase, and illustrate main ideas and points.
☐	☐	I was able to create and give a presentation on a topic.
☐	☐	I successfully outlined a partner's presentation.
☐	☐	I can reduce function words when speaking.
☐	☐	I can correctly use the target vocabulary words from the unit.

Discussion Questions

With a partner or in a small group, discuss the following questions.

1. What do you think is the most interesting aspect of psychology?

2. Think about an important social issue. How would a psychologist be involved in trying to solve the problems related to that issue?

3. Do you think that it is ethically acceptable for companies to use psychologists in marketing products to people? Explain your answer.

UNIT 3

Film Know-How

In this unit, you will
> learn about different jobs people do in making a film.
> increase your understanding of the target academic words for this unit.

LISTENING AND SPEAKING SKILLS
> Recording Definitions
> Facilitating a Group Discussion
> **PRONUNCIATION** Reducing Auxiliary Verbs

Self-Assessment
Think about how well you know each target word, and check (✓) the appropriate column. I have…

TARGET WORDS	never seen this word before.	heard or seen the word but am not sure what it means.	heard or seen the word and understand what it means.	used the word confidently in *either* speaking or writing.
AWL				
advocate				
albeit				
bias				
explicit				
ideology				
implicate				
implicit				
infer				
levy				
🔑 liberal				
🔑 parallel				
reside				
subordinate				
violate				

🔑 Oxford 3000™ keywords

Vocabulary Activities

Word Form Chart			
Noun	**Verb**	**Adjective**	**Adverb**
advocate	advocate	_____	_____
bias	bias	biased unbiased	_____
_____	_____	explicit	explicitly
_____	_____	implicit	implicitly
inference	infer	_____	_____

A. Complete the paragraph below with the target words from the Word Form Chart. Use the correct form and tense of each word.

When watching the news, it is important to listen for _____*bias*_____ in

(1. in favor of one side)

the reporting of a news story. When a reporter states his / her opinion

_____, it is easy to understand which viewpoint he / she is

(2. clearly)

_____. However, many times opinions are stated _____,

(3. supporting)   (4. not directly)

which may make it harder to detect _____. In this case, you may

(5. favoritism)

have to _____ what the reporter's opinion is based on how the

(6. conclude from reasoning)

story is reported. Because of this potential confusion, some people have

_____ for a return to traditional, _____ reporting of the news.

(7. recommended)   (8. balanced)

It's easy to confuse the word *infer* WITH the word *imply*. A speaker may imply something without directly saying it, but a listener infers what the speaker means.

> Based on the reporter's positive reaction, we can **infer** that he supports the policy.

> The reporter seemed to **imply** that the policy was good for education.

CORPUS

B. Complete each sentence with the correct form of either *infer* or *imply*.

1. By saying that a significant amount of unfinished work exists, the article _____*implies*_____ that the project would not be completed this year.

2. Based on your advice, you seem to be _____ that I am the best person for the job. I'm not so sure.

3. Based on their remarks, you can _____ that they will call you back for a second interview.

4. The instructor _____ that I would get a high score in the class when she told me not to worry about my grade.

5. Considering the large size of the home in these ancient ruins, we can _____ that someone wealthy lived here.

C. *Explicit* means "saying something clearly, exactly, and openly." *Implicit* means "suggested without being directly expressed." For each sentence, write *E* for "explicitly stated" or *I* for "implicitly stated."

__I__ 1. It might be beneficial to do the reading before taking the exam.

____ 2. You may not copy this product under any circumstances.

____ 3. To receive your license, you must pass the exam.

____ 4. This study guide helped many other people pass the exam, but I am not allowed to recommend a specific product.

____ 5. The contract is valid for three years only.

D. *Parallel* may mean either "two or more lines that are the same distance apart at every point" or "very similar or taking place at the same time." Complete the chart with a partner.

Things that might be the same distance from your city center	Events that are taking place at the same time in your city this month
two rivers	a soccer game and a concert

E. *Subordinate* means "having less power or authority than someone else in a group or an organization." Complete the sentences with appropriate words and phrases.

1. A regional manager is subordinate to _____ a vice president _____.

2. Oftentimes, _____ are subordinate to their parents.

3. At a university, _____ are subordinate to _____.

4. In government, _____ is subordinate to _____.

About the Topic

A movie set is the place where a film is shot, or recorded. While shooting a film, a director may do several takes, or recordings, of one continous scene in order to get it right. Meanwhile, visual effects are an important part of many movies now. Visual effects often include images that are created by computers. These are usually added after shooting the film.

Before You Listen

Read these questions. Discuss your answers in a small group.

1. When you meet up with your friends, what do you often do for fun?
2. What kinds of films do you watch?
3. In filmmaking, what job interests you most? Explain your answer.

Listen

Read the Listen for Main Ideas activity below. Go online to listen to a podcast called *Behind the Scenes!* The host interviews several people working on the set of a new film.

Listen for Main Ideas

Mark each sentence as *T* (true) or *F* (false). Working with a partner, restate false sentences to make them correct.

__T__ 1. The film is an adventure story.

____ 2. The director has more authority than the producer on everything.

____ 3. A visual-effects artist has complete freedom during the design process.

____ 4. A stunt person's job is not always easy.

____ 5. Background actors are free to do what they want on the set.

NOTE-TAKING SKILL | Recording Definitions

LEARN

A definition tells you the meaning of a word or concept. Speakers often define important words and concepts for their audience. Listen for key phrases that tell you when the speaker is giving a definition.

> Filmmaking **is defined as** the process of creating motion pictures.
>
> Filmmaking **refers to** the production of motion pictures.
>
> A blockbuster film **is characterized by** great commercial success.
>
> A blockbuster film **signifies** great commercial success.

After the key phrase, a speaker will often give information that defines the word he / she is trying to describe.

Word being defined	Key phrase	Defining information
Filmmaking	is defined as	the process of creating motion pictures.

APPLY

A. Listen to the audio again. Match each job with the key phrase it is used with in the audio. Write brief notes about each job in the right column.

Job	Key phrase	Defining information
1. director	characterized as	1. *interprets a story, makes it into a film; responsible for total vision*
2. visual-effects artist	signifies	2. _____ _____ _____
3. stunt person	refers to	3. _____ _____ _____
4. background actor	defined as	4. _____ _____ _____

B. Compare your answers with a partner. Add any additional definitions or details that you think are important.

C. With your partner, define one of the jobs in the chart, using your notes.

D. With your partner, discuss three jobs that are interesting to you. Define each one and share your definitions with the class.

Vocabulary Activities

A. Cross out the word or phrase in parentheses that has a different meaning from the other answers. Use a dictionary to help you understand new words.

1. One (*effect / result / implication / ~~cause~~*) of the new rule was the ability to give more scholarship money to students.

2. The government recently began (*charging / protecting / levying / collecting*) taxes on consumer goods.

3. The (*organizations / occupants / residents / inhabitants*) of the building were delighted by the urban garden project.

4. Meadowbrook is a nice (*residential area / apartment complex / housing area / rural area*).

5. Excellent customer service is a central part of the company's (*philosophy / beliefs / rules / ideology*).

6. If you (*violate / break / disregard / weaken*) the law, you'll be fined $100.

Liberal means "generous or something given in large amounts."

*The restaurant gives customers very **liberal** portions during lunch hours.*

Liberal can also mean "not completely accurate or exact."

*It was a **liberal** translation that changed the meaning of the original work.*

In education, *liberal* means "increasing general knowledge and experience rather than particular skills."

*A **liberal** arts education gives students an opportunity to explore more than one academic interest.*

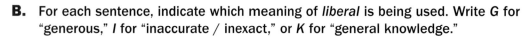

CORPUS

B. For each sentence, indicate which meaning of *liberal* is being used. Write *G* for "generous," *I* for "inaccurate / inexact," or *K* for "general knowledge."

_G_ 1. He used to use a liberal amount of salt on all his food, but now he's watching his blood pressure, so he uses very little salt.

____ 2. The lawyer provided a liberal interpretation of the law in defending his client, in an attempt to get the charges dropped.

____ 3. Although she is liberal with her praise of the students, she expects them to work hard in class.

____ 4. The professor explained the programs offered at a liberal arts college.

____ 5. With a liberal amount of soap, Allen was able to clean the dirt from the floor.

Albeit means "although." However, unlike *although*, *albeit* is never used with a phrase that contains a clause. (Remember, a clause is a phrase that includes a noun and a verb.)

*The printed magazine resembles the online version, **albeit** without links to videos.*

*The printed magazine resembles the online version, **although** it does not include links to videos.*

*The city, **albeit** a small one, has many large buildings of historical importance.*

***Although** the city is small, it has many large buildings of historical importance.*

CORPUS

C. Choose the best phrase on the right that completes each sentence on the left.

_c_ 1. Her blog receives much attention,

a. albeit briefly, during last night's game.

___ 2. Many newspapers are still being printed,

b. albeit in a reduced format.

___ 3. The advertisement,

c. albeit from local people only.

___ 4. Bill Gates attended Harvard,

d. albeit for a short time, in the 1970s.

___ 5. Our team looked like it was going to win,

e. albeit an expensive one, helped attract customers.

D. Choose the target word that best collocates with each group of words below.

implicate	levy	liberal	reside	violate

1. ___liberal___ : quantity, serving, portion, ___amount___

2. _____ : a fine, a tariff, a surcharge, a(n) _____

3. _____ : in a vicinity, in a neighborhood, in a home, at a(n) _____

4. _____ : in a wrongdoing, in a scandal, in an offense, in a(n) _____

5. _____ : the law, standards, a promise, a(n) _____

E. Choose a word from the box below to add to each list of words in activity D.

address	agreement	crime	amount	tax

F. *Levy* means "to use authority to demand and collect a payment," especially a tax. Discuss four things taxes are levied on where you live.

1. _State taxes are levied on personal income in Kentucky._

2. _____

3. _____

4. _____

About the Topic

A documentary film usually tries to report the facts of a real-life situation. For instance, a documentary about urban gardens might seek to explain how people are creating gardens in large cities. Some documentaries are well known for presenting a situation from a specific or unique perspective.

Before You Listen

Read these questions. Discuss your answers in a small group.

1. What types of documentary films are interesting to you?

2. If you were going to make a documentary, what would it be about?

3. How does an international student's experience differ from that of other students' experiences?

Listen

Read the Listen for Main Ideas activity below. Go online to listen to three students discuss an assignment that requires them to make a documentary-style film.

Listen for Main Ideas

Work with a partner to ask and answer the questions below.

1. What is the assignment that the students discuss? *making a documentary*

2. Is the documentary supposed to be a long or short film?

3. How many ideas do the students discuss?

4. What is one of the ideas for the documentary?

SPEAKING SKILL   Facilitating a Group Discussion

LEARN

In class, you may be asked to participate in group discussions. *Facilitating discussions* means to keep the conversation moving and include everyone. Facilitating a discussion includes introducing and concluding the discussion and giving speakers encouragement. Three other skills for facilitating a discussion are listed below, along with some language that you can use with each skill.

First, you want to *guide the discussion*. This means to keep the discussion progressing and not talk about any one thing for too long. Second, facilitating may include *eliciting more details*. This allows the group to learn more about the general idea and to learn about specific examples related to the topic. Third, you should *ensure group participation*. To do this, make sure everyone is involved in the discussion and that a variety of ideas is presented.

Facilitation skill	Useful phrases
Guiding the discussion	• Perhaps we could discuss another possible topic and come back to it … • Why don't we move on. • I think we may have addressed this issue. Let's continue to … • _____ _____
Eliciting more details	• What do you mean exactly? • Could you be more specific about what we would do … ? • Could you give us a concrete example of what you are talking about? • _____ _____
Ensuring group participation	• What's your feeling on it? • What are your thoughts, (Maya)? • What would be your response to that? • _____ _____

APPLY

A. Read the phrases below. Add them to the appropriate box in the chart above.

> Could you specify what you mean?
>
> What do you think about what she just said?
>
> We only have two minutes left. Should we get back to the original topic?

B. Listen to the audio again. Using the chart above, check (✓) the phrases that you hear and compare your answers with a partner.

C. Work in a small group. Think of phrases that you can add to the chart above. Share your answers with the class.

D. In a small group, discuss the topic below. Assign a facilitation skill to each member of the group.

Changing media
Think about how your grandparents and parents got news. Compare the news media of the past with how you learn the news now. What has changed? Do you think the changes are good? Why or why not? How do you think the media might change in the future?

was	/wəz/	**have**		**would**	
were	/wər/	has	/s, z, əz/	/d/	
been	/bən/	have	/v, əv/	/əd/	
being	/bing/			/wəd/	

B. Go online to hear how to reduce *Wh-* words + *do you*. *Whodaya see? Whaddaya do? Whendaya leave? Wheredaya live? Whydaya say that? Howdaya pronounce this?*

C. After a *Wh-* question word, *does* and *did* can have more extreme reductions. Go online to listen and repeat some examples.

does	did
1. Who /dəz/ John report to?	1. Who /d/ ɦe get in touch with?
2. What /s/ this mean?	2. Whaťt /d/ John want?
3. When /z/ the movie start?	3. When /d/ ɦe get here?
4. Where /z/ ɦe live?	4. Where /d/ I put my keys?
5. Why /z/ ɦe do that?	5. Why /d/ ɦe do that?
6. How /z/ this work?	6. How /d/ that happen?

D. Unstressed auxiliaries verbs often sound the same. Look at the chart. Go online to listen to the sentences. Practice them with a partner.

	/s/	/z/	/əz/
is	1. My homework /s/ done.	When /z/ the deadline?	Your English /əz/getting better!
has	2. The clock /s/ stopped.	The dog /z/ disappeared.	My wish /əz/ come true!
does	3. What /s/ this mean?	Who /z/ this belong to?	———————————

	/d/		/əd/
had	4. You /d/ better stop that right now!		John /əd/ been to 14 countries by the time he was ten.
would	5. Mary /d/ do that differently.		I'm sure Bob /ed/ help if you asked.

A. Go online to listen to sentences with reduced auxiliary verbs. Write the sentences using full forms. Check your answers with a partner. Then practice the sentences using reductions.

1. *How have you been?*	9.
2.	10.
3.	11.
4.	12.
5.	13.
6.	14.
7.	15.
8.	16.

B. Work in a small group. Ask your classmates for their opinions about a variety of topics you think are interesting. Use the following phrases to have a conversation.

Whaddaya think about ...	Whydaya think ...
Howdaya feel about ...	Whodaya believe ...
Whendaya consider ...	Wheredaya guess ...

Whaddaya think about people using their cell phones everywhere they go?

End of Unit Task

In this unit, you learned how to listen for and record definitions. You also learned about ways to facilitate a group discussion. Now practice these skills.

A. As a class, divide into two groups. Each group should brainstorm three important city programs or projects such as a citywide recycling program. As you brainstorm, use the facilitation skills that you learned in this unit.

Facilitation skill	Useful phrases
	• Perhaps we could discuss another topic and come back to it later.
	• Why don't we move on.
1. Guiding the discussion	• I think we may have addressed this issue. Let's continue to ...
	• We only have two minutes left. Should we get back to the original topic?

2. Eliciting more details	• What do you mean exactly?
	• But could you be more specific about what we would do?
	• Could you give us a concrete example of what you're talking about?
	• Could you specify what you mean?
3. Ensuring group participation	• What are your thoughts?
	• What's your feeling about it?
	• What would be your response to that?
	• What do you think about what she just said?

B. After you have three ideas, define each one by including defining information related to the idea. Continue to use your facilitation skills.

C. Discuss your three ideas. Assign facilitation skills (1–3) to each member of your group: 1. guiding the discussion, 2. eliciting more details, 3. ensuring group participation.

D. Imagine that the students in your group are city planners. You can only choose one of the group's ideas to implement. Using the facilitation skills that you learned, choose one idea to present to the rest of the class.

E. Discuss your ideas as a class.

1. Explain why your group's idea for the city should be implemented. Make sure that you support your idea.

2. As you listen and participate in the class discussion, check (✓) facilitation skills that you hear in the chart above.

Self-Assessment		
Yes	**No**	
☐	☐	I successfully listened for definitions.
☐	☐	I successfully took notes on the defined words.
☐	☐	I successfully helped facilitate a group discussion.
☐	☐	I was able to participate in a class discussion.
☐	☐	I can reduce auxiliary verbs when speaking.
☐	☐	I can correctly use the target vocabulary words from the unit.

Discussion Questions

With a partner or in a small group, discuss the following questions.

1. In school, which kinds of assignments do you think helped you learn the most?

2. What was the most interesting school or work assignment that you have done?

UNIT 4

Sound Response

In this unit, you will

> learn more about people and their responses to sound.
> increase your understanding of the target academic words for this unit.

LISTENING AND SPEAKING SKILLS

> Cause-and-Effect Relationships
> Citing Sources
> **PRONUNCIATION** Reducing Modal Verbs

Self-Assessment

Think about how well you know each target word, and check (✓) the appropriate column. I have...

TARGET WORDS	never seen this word before.	heard or seen the word but am not sure what it means.	heard or seen the word and understand what it means.	used the word confidently in *either* speaking or writing.
AWL				
adjacent				
🔑 adjust				
cite				
commodity				
empirical				
🔑 federal				
incline				
negate				
orient				
phenomenon				
🔑 pose				
🔑 pursue				
🔑 sex				
🔑 via				

🔑 Oxford 3000™ keywords

Vocabulary Activities

Word Form Chart		
Noun	**Verb**	**Adjective**
_____	_____	adjacent
adjustment	adjust	adjusted
commodity	_____	_____
federation	_____	federal
negative	negate	negative
pose	pose	_____

A. Complete the paragraph below with the target words from the Word Form Chart. Use the correct form and tense of each word. Some words are used more than once.

Some environmentalists say that _commodities_ such as coal should be taxed
      (1. useful items)

by the _____ government. They believe prices should reflect the
    (2. national)

_____ effects of these _____ on the environment. However,
(3. bad)   (4. traded items)

opponents of this strategy argue that _____ prices could _____
         (5. changing)   (6. present)

a threat to the economy. In turn, this could have a(n) _____ effect on
         (7. harmful)

employment, especially in towns and communities _____ to major
       (8. neighboring)

coal-mining operations.

Orient means "to direct someone or something toward" an area of interest.

> This seminar is **oriented** toward people who are interested in photography.

Orient also means "to find your position in relation to your surroundings" or "to make yourself familiar with a new situation."

> During the snowstorm, the driver had difficulty **orienting** himself because it was hard to see.

> It took a long time for me to **orient** myself to the new school.

 CORPUS

B. Check the meaning of *orient* used in each sentence. Write *A* for "area of interest," *P* for "position," or *F* for "familiarity."

_P_ 1. Try to keep the boat oriented toward the shore.

___ 2. Bob is not really oriented toward sports. He doesn't enjoy them much.

_____ 3. Let's see if this map helps us get oriented.

_____ 4. Children learn better when activities are oriented toward things they like to do.

_____ 5. It took a while for Brittany to become oriented with the group. She didn't know anyone there.

Negative is the adjective form of *negate*. It means "bad or harmful" or "lacking enthusiasm or hope."

> Substances that have a **negative** effect on the air and water are referred to as pollutants.

> The outlook for the economy is **negative**. Growth will decline this year.

Negative also refers to scientific results that do not show evidence of a particular condition. Or, it expresses a refusal, or the answer "no."

> The results of the medical tests were **negative**, so Sarah is relieved.

> I received a **negative** reply on my job application.

CORPUS

C. Circle the letter of the word or phrase that best matches the meaning of *negative* used in each sentence.

1. The results of the X-rays came back negative and showed that her broken bone is completely healed.

   (a.) lacking evidence　　　　　b. lacking hope

2. The new video game is fun, but playing for several hours has a negative effect on my eyes.

   a. lacking evidence　　　　　b. harmful

3. Malcolm always gives me a negative response when I ask him for help.

   a. refusal　　　　　b. harmful

4. The team has a very negative attitude about the next game. They don't think they can win.

   a. harmful　　　　　b. lacking enthusiasm

D. *Adjacent* means "next to or near something." Work with a partner to describe the room you are in.

1. The ___whiteboard___ is adjacent to the door.

2. The _____ is adjacent to the _____.

3. My seat is adjacent to _____.

E. A *commodity* is "a product or a raw material that can be bought and sold." Work with a partner to list four more commodities.

1. ___oil___　　　　　4. _____

2. ___water___　　　　5. _____

3. _____　　　6. _____

About the Topic

A decibel is a unit of measurement for sound. Humans speak at 65 decibels. Breathing is about 10 decibels, but a departing plane is about 90 decibels. Higher levels of sound can affect a person's health and blood circulation. Blood circulation is the movement of blood throughout the body.

Before You Listen

Read the following questions. Discuss your answers in a small group.

1. What is your favorite kind of music?
2. What is a positive experience you have had with music?
3. Do you think music can be beneficial? Explain your answer.

🔊 Listen

Read the Listen for Main Ideas activity below. Go online to listen to a weekly show that discusses issues in music. In this episode, the host interviews an expert on using sound, particularly music, to help people.

🔊 Listen for Main Ideas

Mark each sentence as *T* (true) or *F* (false). Work with a partner. Restate false sentences to make them correct.

_T_ 1. The Sound Healing Center uses music to help people improve their lives.

___ 2. Research has shown that music helps people.

___ 3. Noise pollution is annoying, but it does not affect a person's health.

___ 4. It is good to have time for silence every day.

LISTENING SKILL Cause-and-Effect Relationships

LEARN

A *cause* is "what makes something happen." An *effect* is "the result of a cause." In many cases, a speaker can use a *cause signal phrase* at the beginning or in the middle of a sentence.

"The plane was delayed *because* of bad weather."

"*Because of* bad weather, the plane was delayed."

Cause: bad weather → Effect: plane delayed

In lectures, presentations, and discussions, speakers often talk about cause-and-effect relationships to show connections between important points. Look at the signal phrases that show cause-and-effect relationships in the charts on page 41.

Cause signal phrases (reason)	Effect signal phrases (result)
The flight delay was **caused by / due to / attributable to** bad weather.	The weather conditions were extremely poor. **As a result / Consequently**, the flight was delayed.
Because of bad weather, the flight was delayed.	The weather conditions were extremely poor, **causing** the flight to be delayed.
Since the weather conditions were extremely poor, the flight was delayed.	The weather conditions were extremely poor, **resulting** in the flight being delayed.

APPLY

A. For each sentence, circle the cause and underline the effect.

1. Shania's <u>high grades</u> were attributable to (long hours studying)

2. The internship went very well. Consequently, the company offered Lee a full-time position.

3. Price inflation was caused by an increase in the money supply.

B. Work with a partner. Discuss two sentences that you can make using each set of terms and signal phrases.

1. growing economy / more jobs / result in / because of *The growing economy has resulted in more jobs. / Because of the growing economy, there are more jobs.*

2. trained every day for a year / made the team / as a result / since

3. ___ / ___ / due to / resulting in

C. Read the information in the chart below. Then listen to part of the audio again and complete the chart based on the cause-and-effect relationships you hear.

Cause	Effect
1. _____Since_____ we serve so many different purposes,	we have a really wide range of programs ...
2. _____ a well-functioning body.	Our ability to successfully perform tasks at work ... can be at least partly
... there is always movement of people and machines,	3. _____

D. Listen to the last part of the audio again. Work with a partner. Using the notes below and the signal words in the chart at the top of the page, discuss the cause-and-effect relationships that you hear.

1. noise day and night → a person's health *There is a lot of noise day and night. Consequently, this noise can sometimes affect a person's health.*

2. sounds from planes → stress

3. noise from machines around the house → families

Vocabulary Activities

Word Form Chart			
Noun	**Verb**	**Adjective**	**Adverb**
citation	cite	_____	_____
empiricism	_____	empirical	empirically
inclination	incline	inclined	_____
phenomenon	_____	phenomenal	_____
pursuit	pursue	_____	_____
sex	_____	_____	_____

A. Complete the paragraph below with the target words from the Word Form Chart. Use the correct form and tense of each word. Use the words in parentheses to help you. Some words are used more than once.

When scientists observe a surprising *phenomenon*, they are cautious
                                     (1. notable event)

about making bold statements on what it means. Even if they have a strong

_____ about what caused the event, they don't immediately form a
(2. way of feeling)

conclusion. Instead, they wait for _____ evidence, which is obtained
                                    (3. observable)

through scientific experiments that have measurable and observable results.

Even after a study seems to prove what causes a certain _____,
                                                         (4. impressive occurrence)

scientists research other possible variables. For example, suppose

psychologists are testing learning behaviors in rats by having them run

through mazes. If male rats were tested first, scientists might change the

_____ of the test subjects, using female rats next. Most scientists are
(5. gender)

only satisfied after they are able to _____ several independent studies
                                       (6. mention)

supporting the same conclusion. It is true that the _____ of scientific
                                                     (7. search)

truth often requires considerable patience.

B. Some words have multiple meanings. For the target words below, match the dictionary definitions on the left with the example sentences on the right.

cite

Definitions

<u>c</u> 1. to mention something as a reason or an example

___ 2. to speak or write the exact words from a book or author

___ 3. to order someone to appear in court; to mention someone in a legal case

___ 4. to mention someone publicly because they deserve praise

Example Sentences

a. The driver was cited for speeding.

b. The volunteers were cited for their commitment and hard work.

c. Kay cited her 6:00 a.m. appointment tomorrow as an excuse for leaving early this evening.

d. Sam frequently cites lines from Shakespeare to impress his friends.

pursue

Definitions

___ 1. to do something or try to achieve something over a period of time

___ 2. to continue to discuss, research, or be involved in something

___ 3. to follow or chase something or someone, especially to catch the object or person

Example Sentences

a. The police officer pursued the suspect from Chicago to New York.

b. For years, scientists have been pursuing a cure for cancer.

c. I decided not to pursue the scholarship because the application required five essays.

A *phenomenon* is "an event in nature or society, especially one that is not fully understood" or "a person or thing that is very successful." The plural form is *phenomena*.

*The eight-year-old violinist is a huge **phenomenon**.*

*Thunder and lightning are natural **phenomena**.*

The adjective form is *phenomenal*, which means "great," "impressive," or "extraordinary."

*It was a **phenomenal** concert. I really enjoyed it.*

*The dinner that Luis cooked was **phenomenal**.*

CORPUS

C. Complete each sentence with *phenomenon* or *phenomenal.*

1. The Northern Lights were amazing! We had never seen such a <u>*phenomenon*</u> .

2. Several thousands of people had come for what they assumed would be a _____ speech by the former president.

3. A shooting star is a rare _____ .

The preposition *via* means "through a place" or "by means of a particular person, system," or method.

*We flew from Cairo to London **via** Paris.*

*Our furniture was shipped **via** train, which took nearly three weeks.*

CORPUS

D. Select the phrase on the right that best completes each sentence on the left.

_a_ 1. Many banks offer their services   a. via Internet banking.

____ 2. Millions of workers travel to work each day   b. via text message.

____ 3. You can fly to New York from here   c. via subway.

____ 4. For three days, I've been trying to reach her   d. via plane or helicopter.

About the Topic

Tone is the quality of a sound. Mandarin is a tonal language in which the meaning of a word may change based on how high or low a sound is, or on a person's voice pitch. Accent is something different. Accent refers to how someone pronounces a language without affecting the meaning of the words.

Before You Watch

Read these questions. Discuss your answers in a small group.

1. What are some interesting characteristics of your native language(s)?

2. Do you think good musicians are born with natural talent? Explain your answer.

3. What instrument do you think is the most difficult to play?

Watch

Read the Listen for Main Ideas activity below. Go online to watch a presentation about perfect pitch. Based on research, certain factors may determine whether or not someone has perfect pitch.

Listen for Main Ideas

Read the questions about the video. Work with a partner to ask and answer these questions.

1. What age group is most likely to develop perfect pitch? *Those who begin studying music before the age of four are more likely to develop perfect pitch.*

2. Why are Chinese music students more likely to develop perfect pitch?

3. Why does the presenter use the word *ma* as an example?

4. Why is it difficult to learn new sounds later in life?

LEARN

When you give an academic presentation, you need to present evidence that supports the information that you present. This gives you credibility, meaning your audience has reason to believe and trust what you say. An important part of correct citation is acknowledging the sources of any data, quotes, or ideas that you mention. In other words, you should cite your sources. When you cite sources, you also demonstrate that you have thoroughly researched your topic.

Phrases like those in the chart below, signal that you are citing others' work.

Citing sources
[Printed source] demonstrated that ...
In an article published in the [printed source], [person's name] claims ...
A [year] study by [person's name] found ...
According to [person's name], ...
This / My information comes from ...
You can find more information at [website name].

APPLY

A. Read the sentences below. Then watch part of the presentation again and fill in the blanks.

1. The *Psychological Bulletin* ____found____ that adults cannot learn perfect pitch.

2. In an article _____ in the *American Journal of Human Genetics*, Baharloo _____ 600 music students in the U.S. and Europe.

3. Now let's look at a _____ by Diana Deutsch, which appeared in the *Journal of the Acoustical Society of America*.

4. _____ Deutsch, perfect pitch is more common among speakers of tonal languages such as Mandarin and Vietnamese.

5. Deutsch's 2006 experiments _____ through the use of empirical evidence that tonal-language speakers do not vary their pitch.

B. Work with a partner. Using the phrases in the chart above, cite each sentence in Apply activity A in your own words.

According to the Psychological Bulletin, adults cannot learn perfect pitch.

C. Work with a partner. Discuss three kinds of sources that are acceptable for an academic or professional presentation, and two kinds of sources that are not.

LEARN

English speakers reduce modal verbs in both formal and informal situations. Unstressing and reducing these auxiliaries will help you to express yourself clearly.

 A. Go online to listen to reduced modals. Notice that the sentence stress falls on an important content word. The stressed words are written in pink below.

I could do it.	I should do it.	That must be hard.	I must insist!

B. Pronounce *can* and *can't* differently. Go online to listen to four ways to do this.

1. Say /æ/ in *can't*. Say /ə/ in *can*.
   → I **can't** do it. I can do it.

2. Stress *can't*. Unstress *can*.
   → I **can't** do it. I can do it.

3. When *can't* is followed by a consonant, hold your breath instead of making the *t* sound. Then pause briefly.
   → I **can't** | do it.

4. Drop the *t* when *can't* is followed by a vowel sound. Link the word after *can't* with the *n* sound.
   → I **can't** explain it.

C. In fast speech, you reduce the modals. Go online to listen.

	Careful speech	Informal spelling	Everyday reduction
1.	(be) going to	gonna	I'm /gənə/ go.
2.	(has / have) got to	gotta	She's /gədə/ go.
3.	has to	hasta	He /hæstə/ go.
4.	have to	hafta	We /hæftə/ go.
5.	ought to	oughta	You /ədə/ go.
6.	(be) supposed to	supposta, s'posta	I'm /səpoustə, spoustə/ go.

APPLY

A. Go online to listen. Write the sentences you hear with *can* and *can't*.

1. *I can ask.*	6.	
2.	7.	
3.	8.	

4.	9
5.	10.

B. Work with a partner. Ask about plans and obligations. Use the phrasal modals in Learn, activity C.

> A: *Whaddaya gonna do over the weekend?*
>
> B: *I'm gonna do some shopping. What about you?*
>
> A: *I hafta meet a friend at the library on Saturday afternoon. We've gotta study for a quiz.*

End of Unit Task

In this unit, you learned about cause-and-effect relationships and how to cite sources for presentations. Practice these skills by going online to listen to a short podcast about two Voyager spacecraft, which are currently carrying messages from Earth into outer space. Then present the Voyager story, citing sources.

A. As you listen to the podcast, record the cited sources in the chart below.

Paraphrase main ideas	Sources
1. a "golden record" of Earth sounds	1. *the Journal of Space Science*
2. drums, Indian chants, bagpipes + wind, rain, traffic, etc.	2. _____
3. designed to survive for a billion years	3. _____
4. Voyager already passed Jupiter, Saturn, and Neptune	4. _____
5. check for updates	5. _____

B. Compare your sources with a partner.

C. Now use the chart to "present" the Voyager story to your partner, mentioning all of the main ideas and citing sources, using examples from the chart on page 45. On your own chart, put a check mark (✓) next to each idea and source that your partner mentions.

D. Work with a partner. Use the cause-and-effect signal phrases in the chart and the pairs of ideas below it to discuss different aspects of the Voyager spacecraft.

Cause signal phrases	Effect signal phrases
caused by	as a result
due to	consequently
attributable to	causing
because of	resulting in
since	

Example: different languages and sounds from Earth / the golden record

Since NASA wanted to send different languages and sounds from Earth, the golden record was created.

1. an alien civilization might find them / golden records designed to survive for a billion years
2. updates on voyager.jpl.nasa.gov / the spaceship's distance from Earth

	Self-Assessment	
Yes	**No**	
☐	☐	I successfully cited sources using a variety of citation expressions.
☐	☐	I successfully discussed cause-and-effect relationships in my own words.
☐	☐	I recognized and recorded the sources cited by the speaker.
☐	☐	I can reduce modal verbs when speaking.
☐	☐	I can correctly use the target vocabulary words from the unit.

Discussion Questions

With a partner or in a small group, discuss the following questions.

1. What kinds of traditional music do people listen to in your country?
2. In your country, does the younger generation listen to different music from the older generation?
3. Do you think it is OK to download music from the Internet without paying for it? Explain your answer.

UNIT 5

Changing Your Brain

In this unit, you will

> learn about how the brain can change and repair itself.
> increase your understanding of the target academic words for this unit.

LISTENING AND SPEAKING SKILLS

> Listening for Signal Phrases
> Expressing and Responding to an Opinion
> **PRONUNCIATION** Reducing Past Modals

Self-Assessment

Think about how well you know each target word, and check (✓) the appropriate column. I have…

TARGET WORDS	never seen this word before.	heard or seen the word but am not sure what it means.	heard or seen the word and understand what it means.	used the word confidently in *either* speaking or writing.
AWL				
🔑 channel				
constitute				
discriminate				
distort				
invoke				
mode				
nonetheless				
🔑 panel				
predominant				
radical				
suspend				
🔑 trace				
underlie				
🔑 whereas				

🔑 Oxford 3000™ keywords

Vocabulary Activities

Word Form Chart			
Noun	**Verb**	**Adjective**	**Adverb**
channel	channel	_____	_____
constitution	constitute	constitutional	constitutionally
predominance	predominate	predominant	predominantly
trace	trace	traceable	_____

A. Complete the paragraph below with the target words from the Word Form Chart. Use the correct form and tense of each word.

Neuroscientists have ____*traced*____ improvements in functions of the brain to
           (1. discovered by investigation)

"brain exercise." By spending about 30 minutes a day exercising your brain,

it seems you can improve your mental performance. For this reason, some

new websites help you to exercise different _____ of your brain. The
                      (2. systems of communication)

exercises _____ focus on memory, concentration, and speed. Such
         (3. mainly)

websites _____ an increasing number of Internet applications used
       (4. combine to form)

to improve thinking and mental performance.

Mode is "a particular way of doing something" or a "way of feeling or behaving." We often use *mode* with the preposition *of*.

Customers may choose their preferred **mode of** *payment. We accept cash, credit cards, debit cards, and checks.*

CORPUS

B. Complete the following chart. Compare your answers with a partner.

What is your preferred ...	You
mode of transportation?	_____
mode of communication when you need to discuss a group project for work or school?	_____
mode of instruction in class?	_____
mode of payment when you eat at a restaurant?	_____

C. Read the variations on one of the definitions of *panel*. Then write the letter that best matches the way *panel* is used in the sentences below.

> a. a group selected for a specific service
>
> b. a group of people who discuss a topic in front of an audience

_a_ 1. The panel of professors debated the new admission policy.

____ 2. The police brought a panel of experts to the station to help them solve the crime.

____ 3. Last night, a panel of four officials discussed the city's traffic problems at the university auditorium.

D. *Whereas* connects two ideas that contrast with each other. *Predominantly* means "mainly." Complete the sentences below. Discuss your answers with a partner.

1. People in my country predominantly eat _____ *fish* _____, whereas people in _____ *Mongolia* _____ predominantly eat _____ *beef* _____.

2. Homes in my country are predominantly made of _____, whereas homes in _____ are predominantly made of _____.

3. People in my country predominantly speak _____, whereas people in _____ predominantly speak _____.

The word *channel* has several different meanings. It can refer to a television or radio station.

> *Please change the **channel**, so we can watch something else.*

Channel can also refer to a means of communication or distribution.

> *The company uses its stores, website, and other distribution **channels** to sell its product.*

It can mean "a way of expressing ideas and feelings."

> *Painting is a **channel** some artists use to express ideas and feelings.*

A *channel* can also refer to a route or waterway between two bodies of water.

> *The Suez Canal is a major **channel** between the Mediterranean Sea and Red Sea.*

CORPUS

E. Circle the correct meaning for *channel(s)* in each sentence.

1. A signal is sent through channels in the brain, telling the body what to do. ((means of communication) / *way to express feeling*)

2. A large channel separates England and France. (*a TV station* / *a waterway*)

3. Bank loans are one channel that new businesses can use to borrow money. (*way to express feeling* / *means of distribution*)

4. One way to avoid stress is to channel all of your tension into exercise. (*means of distribution* / *expression of ideas*)

About the Topic

A neuroscientist studies the body's nervous system. The nervous system passes signals between the brain and the rest of the body. Neurons are cells that transmit information that is needed for the brain and body to function properly. Over time, neurons form neural pathways.

Before You Listen

Read these questions. Discuss your answers in a small group.

1. What is one good habit you have? What is one bad habit that you have?
2. Why do you think people often have a hard time changing their bad habits?
3. Do you think that it is possible for older people to change their habits?

Listen

Read the Listen for Main Ideas activity below. Go online to listen to an interview on a television show about health. A neuroscientist discusses how we can change and even repair our brains.

Listen for Main Ideas

Mark each sentence as *T* (true) or *F* (false). Work with a partner. Restate false sentences to make them correct.

___ 1. New experiences and thinking can change the brain.

___ 2. Habits that are repeated create weaker channels in the brain.

___ 3. Today, neuroscientists believe the brain stops developing after a person becomes an adult.

___ 4. Stress damages the brain.

LISTENING SKILL   Listening for Signal Phrases

LEARN

A *signal phrase* is a word or group of words that tell the listener what kind of information is going to come next. Paying attention to signal phrases will help you follow lectures, presentations, interviews, and other forms of formal discussions. Look at the examples in the chart below.

Purpose	Signal phrases
Main ideas or sequence	**At the outset,** I would like to mention the effects of stress ...
	As a final point, you should try to exercise your brain every day.
	To begin with,

Examples	**To illustrate the idea**, reading new material can produce changes … **To elucidate this point**, the research showed that reading about an exciting new technology can create new channels in the brain. _____
Additional ideas	**Additionally**, exercising your brain can improve mental performance. **Along with this**, your general health will improve. _____
Contrasting ideas	The neuroscience program offers students excellent opportunities. **On the other hand**, it takes five years to complete. I like speed exercises, **whereas** my friend enjoys memory games. _____
Emphasis	**It is important to remember that** some habits are hard to change. Neurons are located **not only** in the brain **but also** in the body. _____

APPLY

A. Review the signal phrases in the box below. Add them to the chart above in the appropriate section.

For instance	However	To begin with
Furthermore	It's crucial to understand that	

B. Read the sentences below. Then go online to listen to part of the audio. Write the signal phrases that you hear, and identify the type of signal phrase used.

1. So, ___to illustrate this___, when you learn something new while reading a book, your brain changes. _____Examples_____

2. _____, when you repeat an activity or a thought, the brain's connections become stronger over time. _____

3. Scientists have traced everyday habits and activities to the creation of very strong channels in the brain for _____ good habits, _____ unhealthy ones. _____

4. In the past, the predominant view among neuroscientists was that once a person became an adult, the brain stopped developing, _____ today neuroscientists know the brain can change at any age.

   _____

5. With that said, _____ that it's harder to change if a person has had the same habits for a long time … . _____

Vocabulary Activities

A. Cross out the word in parentheses that has a different meaning from the other answers. Use a dictionary to help you understand new words.

1. The (*underlying / ultimate / central / ~~complex~~*) reason for the company's success was its ability to attract talent from all over the world.

2. The program is unable to (*distinguish / differentiate / discover / discriminate*) between commands. We need to fix it.

3. The mirror (*distorted / misrepresented / altered / revised*) the shape of everyone's body, making us appear enormously tall.

4. The lawyer (*cited / invoked / imitated / mentioned*) the new law while defending his client.

5. The game was (*suspended / ended / postponed / delayed*) because of the rain. The teams will play tomorrow instead.

B. Match the definitions on the left with the example sentences on the right.

| discriminate |

Definitions

__C__ 1. to recognize or show a difference between people or things

____ 2. to unfairly treat one person or group better or worse than others

____ 3. to be able to judge the quality of something

Example Sentences

a. The local agency had a record of discriminating against people from other regions of the country.

b. If you buy something in the market, you must be able to discriminate between good and bad quality items.

c. I've often wondered how scientists are able to discriminate between male and female fish.

| radical |

Definitions

____ 1. thorough and complete; concerning the important and basic parts of something

____ 2. new; different; likely to have a great effect

Example Sentences

a. After the evaluation, the government announced a radical review of its procedures.

b. Electric cars represent a radical change from gas-fueled automobiles.

Nonetheless means "despite this fact."

> *Christy's new job is really difficult;* **nonetheless**, *she says that it is quite rewarding.*

CORPUS

C. Select the best phrase to complete each sentence.

1. Jim spent an hour cleaning his room. Nonetheless, _d_
2. Nora has a college degree. Nonetheless, ____
3. Sarah seemed convincing. Nonetheless, ____
4. Tony's ideas are really different. Nonetheless, ____

a. most of his colleagues seem to like them.
b. she is having difficulty finding a job.
c. very few people agreed with her.
d. it still looked messy.

Distort means "to change the shape, appearance, or sound of something so that it is strange or not clear."

*The microphone **distorted** his voice, making him hard to understand.*

Distort also means "to twist or change facts and ideas so that they are no longer true."

*The news report **distorted** the event, making it seem much bigger than it actually was.*

CORPUS

D. List examples of different kinds of *distortions* in the chart.

Things that distort a person's shape, sound, or appearance	Things that can be distorted so that they are no longer true
a microphone	a news report

E. *Underlie* means "to be the basis or cause of something." Rank some of the underlying reasons for professional success (1 = most important, 6 = least important). Compare your answers with a partner.

Underlying reasons for a person's success	Rank
effort	____
natural talent	____
background	____
personality	____
connections	____
passion	____

About the Topic

The definition of *intelligence* is somewhat controversial. Many tests exist that are designed to measure intelligence. The IQ test is the traditional test of intelligence. Multiple intelligences tests are another type of intelligence test. They are designed to test different aspects of intelligence, or ways of learning, including interpersonal, spatial, and bodily-kinesthetic to name a few.

Before You Watch

Read the questions below. Discuss your answers in a small group.

1. How would you define intelligence?
2. What is the best measure of a person's intelligence?
3. Does intelligence equal success in life?

Watch

Read the Listen for Main Ideas activity below. Go online to watch three students discuss the meaning of *intelligence* during a study session.

Listen for Main Ideas

Mark each sentence as *T* (true) or *F* (false). Work with a partner. Restate false sentences to make them correct.

_T_ 1. The students have different opinions about what intelligence is.

___ 2. According to all three students, learning ability is the most important type of intelligence.

___ 3. The students disagree about the use of IQ tests to measure intelligence.

___ 4. The term *multiple intelligences* refers to different kinds of intelligence.

SPEAKING SKILL   Expressing and Responding to an Opinion

LEARN

At some point, you may need to participate in formal discussions at school or in the workplace. During formal discussions, you will need to express your opinion to colleagues or a small or large group.

Phrases for expressing an opinion
From my point of view, this is ...
As far as I am concerned, it is ...
To be honest, I would argue that ...

When you respond to an opinion, you should do it calmly and politely.

When you *partially agree*, you disagree or agree with only part of something. Partially agreeing shows your understanding of others' opinions. It also allows you to focus on key points that you disagree with.

Remaining neutral means that you do not agree or disagree. You remain neutral if you have not formed your opinion yet or if you want to hear more before you form your own opinion.

Phrases for responding to an opinion		
Disagreeing politely	**Partially agreeing**	**Remaining neutral**
I understand what you are saying, but …	I'm in agreement with you for the most part. Except, …	I'm still trying to determine how I feel about it.
I view it somewhat differently.	To some extent, you are right. However, …	I haven't made up my mind yet.
I'm not entirely sure that I agree.	I partially agree with you, but …	I'd like to hear more before I decide.

APPLY

A. Go online to watch the video again. Write a check mark (✓) each time a student expresses or responds to an opinion. It is possible to have more than one check mark for each category.

	Lin	Sam	Blake
Expressing an opinion			
Disagreeing politely			
Partially agreeing			
Remaining neutral			

B. Compare your answers with a partner. Which phrases did you hear?

C. Read the opinions below. Working with a partner, express and respond to each statement. Use phrases from the charts above.

1. "Intelligence is the ability to learn and solve problems quickly."

2. "There are several different types of intelligence, like artistic, musical, and emotional intelligences."

3. "I think IQ tests are the best way to [test intelligence]."

D. Work in a small group. Discuss the following question:

What is the most important type of intelligence to have?

LEARN

Past modals, such as *would have* and *should not have*, are unstressed function words. Like other auxiliary verbs, you reduce them in speech. Function words are considered less important than content words. Unstressing these words will improve your English rhythm.

A. Look at the chart. Go online and listen to reduced forms of past modal verbs.

Past Modal	Contraction	Reduction	Tips
could (not) have	could've	coulda	1. *Could've* sounds like *could of*.
	couldn't've	couldena	
would (not) have	would've	woulda	2. Hold your breath instead of making the *t* sound in *might not've*. Then pause briefly before saying the next syllable: maɪt ˌ nɑdə
	wouldn't've	wouldena	
should (not) have	should've	shoulda	
	shouldn't've	shouldena	
must (not) have	must've	musta	3. Let the air out of your nose when you say *d* in *couldena*, *wouldena*, *shouldena*.
	must not've	musnada	
may (not) have	may've	maya	
	may not've	maynada	
might (not) have	might've	mighta	
	might not've	mightnada	

B. Go online to listen to past modals in sentences. The main stress falls on important content words. Those words are pink in the chart below.

Modal + Consonant → Drop /v/		Modal + Vowel → Link with /v/	
You coulda tried.	You couldena tried.	You coulda ͮ asked.	You couldena ͮ asked.
You woulda liked it.	You wouldena liked it.	He woulda ͮ understood.	He wouldena ͮ understood.
I shoulda said so.	I shouldena said that.	I shoulda ͮ agreed.	I shouldena ͮ agreed.
He musta known.	He musnada known.	He musta ͮ opened it.	He musnada ͮ opened it.
She maya forgotten.	She maynada forgotten.	We maya ͮ answered it.	We maynada ͮ answered it.
They mighta come.	They mightnada come.	They mighta ͮ eaten it.	They mightnada ͮ eaten it.

A. Work with a group. Share true stories about moments you regret. Listen to your classmates and offer alternatives. Consider what they or you could have done differently in various situations.

Tell about a time when you ...

didn't follow your intuition / said the wrong thing / yelled at someone / missed an important opportunity / were accidentally rude to someone / hung up on someone

> A: There was this time when a friend and I were robbed. She had set down her backpack to take a picture, when two guys ran up to us and then ran off with her camera. I shoulda warned her about leaving her stuff on the ground.
>
> B: You coulda offered to hold her bag.
>
> C: I woulda run after those guys and gotten her camera back!
>
> B: I wouldena done that. That's way too dangerous! I woulda just screamed for help.

B. Work with a group. Talk about the situations below. What do you think happened?

Jane's late.	My wallet's missing.
She musta been held up at work.	She got a high score on the exam.
She maya gotten stuck in traffic.	He got into a good graduate school.
She coulda missed her train.	She hasn't gotten back from vacation yet.
She mighta stopped at the store.	He just bought a house in an expensive neighborhood.

End of Unit Task

In this unit, you learned how to listen for signal phrases. You also learned how to express and respond to an opinion. Practice these skills by creating a short presentation. Then discuss your presentation with another group.

A. Work in groups of four. Develop a group opinion on a current issue or topic of debate. For example, you could use one of the categories from the chart below or come up with your own topic.

Category	Sample topic
New laws	Giving fines for not recycling
Urban projects	Using government funds to turn city rooftops into urban gardens
Health concerns	Taxing the consumption of caffeinated beverages
Education issues	Providing more technical education in high schools

B. Present your opinion by assigning one role to each member of the group. Use at least one signal word from each category listed below.

Main ideas or sequence	At the outset, As a final point, To begin with,	Contrasting ideas	On the other hand, ... , whereas However,
Examples	To illustrate this idea, To elucidate this point, For instance,	Emphasis	It is important to remember that ... ... not only ... but also ... It is crucial to understand that ...
Additional ideas	Additionally, Along with this, Moreover,		

I. Introduction – (Student 1)

II. Body

      A. – (Student 2)

      B. – (Student 3)

III. Conclusion – (Student 4)

C. Share your presentation with another group. As you listen to the other group's presentation, check the signal phrases that you hear.

D. Discuss the presentations with your group and the group you presented to. Use the expressions you learned for expressing and responding to an opinion.

		Self-Assessment
Yes	**No**	
☐	☐	I learned to listen for signal phrases.
☐	☐	I was able to express my opinion and respond to other opinions.
☐	☐	I reduced emphasis on past modal verbs when speaking.
☐	☐	I can correctly use the target vocabulary words from the unit.

Discussion Questions

With a partner or in a small group, discuss the following questions.

1. Do you think scientists will ever be able to completely map the brain?

2. What is the most interesting aspect of the human brain to you?

UNIT 6

Micro Approach, Macro Improvement

In this unit, you will

> learn about the phenomenon of microcredit.
> increase your understanding of the target academic words for this unit.

LISTENING AND SPEAKING SKILLS

> Inferences
> Checking for Understanding
> **PRONUNCIATION** Linking Consonants: *ch*, *j*, *sh*, and *zh*

Self-Assessment

Think about how well you know each target word, and check (✓) the appropriate column. I have...

TARGET WORDS	never seen this word before.	heard or seen the word but am not sure what it means.	heard or seen the word and understand what it means.	used the word confidently in *either* speaking or writing.
AWL				
aggregate				
constrain				
🔑 contemporary				
domain				
🔑 export				
framework				
hierarchy				
integral				
integrate				
🔑 ministry				
notwithstanding				
🔑 prospect				
🔑 sector				
sphere				

🔑 Oxford 3000™ keywords

Vocabulary Activities

The nouns *domain*, *sector*, and *sphere* have similar meanings. When they are used with the word *public*, their meanings are more distinct.

Domain means "an area of knowledge or activity, especially one that someone is responsible for."	*Public domain* refers to works that are publicly available. Anyone can access them.
Sector means "a part of an area or activity, especially of a country's economy," such as an industry.	The *public sector* is the part of the economy that provides basic government services. The police are part of the public sector.
Sphere means "an area of activity, influence, or interest; a particular section of society."	The *public sphere* is an area of social life in which people discuss issues and opinions. An online discussion group is an example of the public sphere.

A. Complete each sentence with *domain*, *sector*, or *sphere*.

1. In many countries, the health system is part of the public ____sector____ and is supported by the government.

2. When an author's ownership rights to his / her music or literature expire, the work of art may enter the public _____ .

3. Good nutrition is a frequent topic of discussion in the public _____ even though people have different opinions about what foods are healthy.

4. As patents expire, the formulas for new medications will eventually enter the public _____ . After that, other companies can begin to manufacture them.

Aggregate means "to put together different items and amounts into a single group or total."

> *The computer **aggregated** all of the phone fees for the entire year.*

Integrate means "to combine two or more things so they work together."

> *The company decided to **integrate** the sales and marketing departments into one large department.*

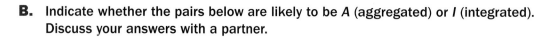
CORPUS

B. Indicate whether the pairs below are likely to be *A* (aggregated) or *I* (integrated). Discuss your answers with a partner.

__A__ 1. a company / sales for the year

____ 2. a community / immigrants

____ 3. all data from a survey / a year-end report

____ 4. new students / school

____ 5. a hi-tech computer system / a company's computer network

____ 6. total exports / a country

____ 7. bank deposits / the sum of a person's income

aggregate	constraint	integrate	sector

C. Complete the paragraph below using the target words from the box. Use the correct form and tense of each word.

In recent years, some economists have called for greater economic

integration between the public and private _____. They believe
(1. combining)   (2. areas)

that this is necessary to increase the _____ efficiency of a country's
                                          (3. total)

economy. However, one _____ to economic _____ is
                         (4. limitation)   (5. incorporation)

disagreement over how to _____ the different parts of the economy.
                            (6. unite)

Integral is an adjective that means "being an essential (or important) part of something." It is used to express how a part relates to a whole.

> A shared sense of responsibility is **integral** to the success of a community.
>   part   whole

> Reliability is an **integral** aspect of teamwork.
>   part   whole

CORPUS

D. Use the words and phrases in parentheses to complete the sentences.

1. Form is an integral element of _____art_____. (form / art)

2. Regular _____ is integral to overall good _____.
   (health / exercise)

3. Some economists claim that _____ is an integral component of
   _____. (financial gain / risk)

4. _____ is integral to a successful _____. (practice /
   performance)

5. Both _____ and _____ are integral aspects of _____.
   (intonation / communication / gestures)

6. _____ can play an integral role in a person's _____.
   (professional success / networking)

About the Topic

A loan is money that a bank lends to a person. When someone wants a loan, a bank will often check that person's credit history to assess risk. If that person has paid his / her debts in the past, he / she will normally have a good credit history. Therefore, loaning money to someone with a good credit history is less of a risk for the bank.

Before You Watch

Read the following questions. Discuss your answers in a small group.

1. If you were going to open a new business, what kind of business would you start?

2. What do you think is the hardest part of owning and operating a business?

3. What is the most successful industry in your country? Explain your answer.

Watch

Read the Listen for Main Ideas activity below. Go online to watch a podcast about how microcredit is helping people around the world create new lives for themselves.

Listen for Main Ideas

Mark each sentence as *T* (true) or *F* (false). Work with a partner. Restate false sentences to make them correct.

_T_ 1. Microcredit is the process of providing small loans to people who normally would not be able to get a bank loan.

____ 2. The Grameen Bank has been in decline since it opened.

____ 3. The use of microcredit is growing in Africa.

____ 4. One problem with microcredit is that there is no incentive to repay the loan.

LISTENING SKILL   Inferences

LEARN

You make an inference when you decide that something is probably true based on the information that you have. Being able to make inferences is important because not all information is explicitly stated. When you make an inference, think about the speaker's opinion, attitude, and tone. Also, ask yourself what the speaker's purpose or area of interest is. Look at the example below.

"As a doctor, I say <u>regular health checks are no laughing matter</u>. I suggest going to see your local medical practitioner once a year. Regular check-ups can help prevent serious problems from developing."

The speaker is a doctor, promoting the importance of health checks. Based on this information, we can reasonably infer that the statement "regular health checks are no laughing matter" means that getting a regular check-up is an important thing to do.

APPLY

A. Go online to watch a part of the video again. What can we infer about the following statements based on the surrounding conversation?

1. "They don't care who you are."

   a. It doesn't matter what kind of business you have.

   b. It doesn't matter how much money you have.

   c. It doesn't matter what kind of person you are.

2. "That's quite an issue."

   a. The effect of microcredit is a debated issue.

   b. The effect of microcredit is a serious issue.

   c. Microcredit is a big issue.

B. Read the statements below. Go online to watch the last part of the video again. Fill out the Notes and Inference columns based on what you hear.

Statement	Notes	Inference
1. "Microcredit is hope."	- rural areas - one-, two-hundred-dollar loan - start a new _____	For people in rural areas with perhaps few opportunities, a microcredit loan can help them start new businesses, which gives them hope for a better future.
2. "The Grameen Bank in Bangladesh is what really got things going."	_____ _____ _____	_____ _____ _____
3. "That's what I call strategy."	_____ _____	_____ _____

C. Work with a partner. Discuss the inferences you made about Statements 2 and 3 in the chart above.

D. Work with a partner to discuss the question below.

On the first day of this class, what did you infer about the following items?

1. the instructor

2. the difficulty of the course

3. the other students in the class

Vocabulary Activities

A. The words *framework* and *hierarchy* have multiple meanings. Match the dictionary definitions on the left with the example sentences on the right.

hierarchy

Definitions

_b_ 1. a system in society or an organization with people arranged in different levels of importance, from high to low

___ 2. a group of people in charge of a large organization

___ 3. a system that ideas or beliefs can be arranged into

Example Sentences

a. Maslow's hierarchy of human needs ranges from shelter and food to personal satisfaction.

b. The public health hierarchy ranges from governmental leaders to volunteer health workers.

c. In many large companies, those at the top of the managerial hierarchy make major decisions.

framework

Definitions

___ 1. the parts of a building or an object that support its weight and give it shape

___ 2. a set of beliefs, ideas, or rules used as the basis for making judgments or decisions

___ 3. the structure of a particular system

Example Sentences

a. The news organization operates under a hierarchical framework.

b. The framework for the bank's new loan program clarifies who is qualified for a loan and who is not.

c. After the framework is complete, the electrical system will be installed.

Prospect has several meanings. It can mean (a) "the possibility (or idea) that something will happen." The adjective is *prospective*.

The opportunity to own my own business is an exciting **prospect**.

The **prospective** homebuyer measured the rooms in the house.

Prospect can also mean (b) "a person (or group) who is likely to be successful in a competition." The plural form is *prospects*, which refers to (c) "the chances of being successful."

There were many applicants, but none of them is a **prospect** for the job.

Without a university education, Joe's **prospects** for finding a job aren't very good.

CORPUS

B. Write the correct form of *prospect* in each sentence. Then write *a, b,* or *c* to show which meaning of prospect is used in each sentence.

_c_ 1. The ministry's goal is to eliminate poverty, but I'm skeptical about its ___prospects___ for doing so.

___ 2. The young golfer looks like a good _____ to win the tournament.

___ 3. _____ business owners must get a license from the ministry in order to operate.

___ 4. The _____ of being my own boss someday motivates me to learn how to run a business.

The adjective *contemporary* means "from the same time" or "modern."

The museum's collection consists of **contemporary** *art from this year.*

CORPUS

C. Rank the following items based on your level of interest in them. Discuss your answers with a partner and give one example of each item.

	(1 = the most interesting, 4 = the least interesting)	Example
contemporary art		
contemporary music		
contemporary architecture		
contemporary literature		

constrain	framework	hierarchy	ministry	notwithstanding

D. Complete the paragraph with the correct forms of the target words from the box.

A new ___framework___ for illness prevention in local communities, based on
     (1. structure)

collaboration between the education system and health care providers has

been put in place. All students will be required to get vaccinated before they

can attend school. A _____ consisting of officials from participating
     (2. ordered group of people in charge)

_____ has been established to oversee the program. Additionally,
(3. government agencies)

doctors will face _____ on what they can charge patients for
     (4. restrictions)

vaccinations. _____ these changes to the fee structure, doctors have
     (5. despite)

enthusiastically supported the program.

About the Topic

When banks lend money to people, they give them money, or a loan, that must be paid back over a period of time. People who take a loan from these banks have to pay interest on the loan. Interest is extra money that is charged to people as they pay back a loan over time.

Before You Listen

Read the questions below. Discuss your answers in a small group.

1. Which charities, businesses, or organizations do you think do a good job of helping people?

2. What do you believe is the best way to help someone in need?

3. In the past ten years, what programs or ideas have greatly improved people's lives?

Listen

Read the Listen for Main Ideas activity below. Go online to listen to a radio program. The host and guest discuss the concept of microlending.

Listen for Main Ideas

Circle the letter of the best answer to complete each sentence.

1. Microlending can be ___.

   a. an online loan from an individual

   b. a traditional bank loan

   c. a high-interest loan from a big bank

2. In microlending, field partners ___.

   a. run people's businesses

   b. work for traditional banks

   c. come from the local community

3. A person who wants to borrow money through this kind of microlending system ___.

   a. sets up a profile online

   b. sends emails out

   c. visits potential lenders

4. The repayment rate for many microloans is ___.

   a. debated by government officials

   b. quite high

   c. lower than that of traditional banks

LEARN

When you check for understanding, you restate what you have heard in your own words. Checking for understanding lets you (1) see if you understood correctly, (2) highlight important points, and (3) clarify details.

Sample phrases for checking for understanding
I just want to make sure that I've got this straight. What you're saying is …
So, if I understand it correctly, …   Let me make sure that I understand.
Now you mentioned that … , right?   So, in essence, what you're telling us is …

After checking for understanding, you will often want to ask follow-up questions to get more information or emphasize the point of clarification.

Sample phrases for follow-up questions
What do you generally do in that situation?   Is that what you wanted to point out?
Is that a fair characterization of your idea?   What is the next step in the process?

APPLY

A. **Discuss the statements below with a partner. Use sample phrases from the chart above to check for understanding.**

1. "Student test scores might not be the only way to judge a school's performance." *So, if I understand you correctly, exam results are not the only factor in determining a school's performance.*

2. "Traveling gave me deeper insight into not only the world but also my own culture."

3. "Microcredit helps people who would not normally be able to receive a loan get a loan for their businesses."

B. **Work with a partner. What follow-up question would you ask for each statement in activity A? Use the phrases in the chart to help you.**

C. **Go online to listen to part of the interview again. Fill in the chart below.**

Checking for understanding	Follow-up questions
1. I just want to make sure that I've got this straight. *What you're saying is* that someone who needs money for a business can simply go online to a microlending site.	2. Is that _____ ?
3. So, _____ , someone can get help from a field partner to set up a profile …	4. _____ the lenders get in return?

LEARN

Connecting the *y* sound with other consonants can result in sound changes.

A. Go online to listen. Notice the new sounds in the word connections.

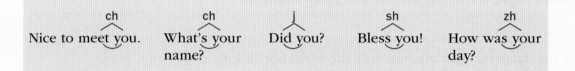

		ch		sh	zh
ch			j		
Nice to meet you.	What's your name?	Did you?	Bless you!	How was your day?

APPLY

A. Go online to listen. Check (✓) the sound you hear.

	ch	sh	j	zh
1. I miss you.	☐	✓	☐	☐
2. Is that your phone?	☐	☐	☐	☐
3. He has your car keys.	☐	☐	☐	☐
4. Would you like some tea?	☐	☐	☐	☐
5. What's your email address?	☐	☐	☐	☐
6. I wish you wouldn't do that.	☐	☐	☐	☐
7. Did you change your password?	☐	☐	☐	☐

B. Go online to listen to some two-line dialogues. You will hear extreme reductions and linking with *ch, j, sh,* and *zh.* On a separate piece of paper, write down a few of the conversations. Listen again to check what you wrote. Then practice saying some of the lines with a partner.

C. Work with a partner. Person A, present a problem. Person B, make a suggestion. Use *Why don't you* … or its extreme reduction, *Whyncha* …

A: I don't know what to do tonight.

B: Why don't you go to a movie?

A: I went to a movie last night.

B: Then why don't you go to a concert?

A: I don't really like concerts.

B: Why don't you go out for dinner, then?

A: Yeah! That sounds good. Great idea!

Problems	
I get bad headaches.	I never have any money!
I'm lonely.	I'm so stressed out!
I'm always tired.	I don't have any friends.
My neighbors are so noisy!	I can't get myself to exercise.
I can't sleep at night.	What should I do with my life?
I hate my job!	I'm bored.

D. Work with a partner. Practice short questions and answers with *wh-* words + *did you.* Use the *j* sound. Make reductions. Notice the informal spelling.

Everyday reductions:	Whodija, Whadija, Whendija, Wheredija, Whydija, Howdija
Fast speech:	Whoja, Whaja, Whenja, Whereja, Whyja, Howja

Whoja go to the movies with?

I went with my sister.

End of Unit Task

In this unit, you learned how to make inferences when listening and you learned how to check for understanding. Review these skills by telling your group about an organization that you are interested in.

A. Find information about an organization or think about one you are familiar with. This organization may be a large company, an international aid group, or another organization that interests you.

Gather information about the organization. Use the Internet, library, or other resources. The questions below will help you do your research.

• What is the organization's main purpose?

• How does the organization operate?

• What countries or regions does the organization serve? What is its size?

- Why is the organization interesting?

- What kinds of projects does the organization support?

- What successes or difficulties has the organization had?

B. Create an outline to organize the information that you found.

I.

II.

III.

C. Work in a small group. Take turns discussing the organizations you researched.

D. As you listen to each member of your group, write notes on something that you would like to check for understanding on. Then prepare a follow-up question.

Self-Assessment		
Yes	**No**	
☐	☐	I was able to make inferences.
☐	☐	I used different phrases to check for understanding.
☐	☐	I asked follow-up questions after checking for understanding.
☐	☐	I can link consonants, especially *ch, j, sh,* and *zh,* and use *wh-* words.
☐	☐	I can correctly use the target vocabulary words from the unit.

Discussion Questions
With a partner or in a small group, discuss the following questions.

1. What is the most complex part of the global economy?

2. Which products or services are done most efficiently by the government (for example, the building of roads) or by private companies (for example, the manufacturing of clothing)?

3. Are there ever any situations in which a person or organization should ignore the economic costs of something?

UNIT 7

Nature or Nurture

In this unit, you will

> learn how language can shape how we experience the world.
> increase your understanding of the target academic words for this unit.

LISTENING AND SPEAKING SKILLS

> Telegraphic Language
> Summarizing Academic Research
> **PRONUNCIATION** Chunking, Pausing, and Intonation

Self-Assessment

Think about how well you know each target word, and check (✓) the appropriate column. I have…

TARGET WORDS	never seen this word before.	heard or seen the word but am not sure what it means.	heard or seen the word and understand what it means.	used the word confidently in *either* speaking or writing.
AWL				
ambiguous				
amend				
arbitrary				
coherent				
conceive				
immigrate				
inherent				
intrinsic				
norm				
presume				
🔑 promote				
🔑 retain				
thereby				
thesis				

🔑 Oxford 3000™ keywords

Word Form Chart			
Noun	**Verb**	**Adjective**	**Adverb**
amendment	amend	_____	_____
coherence	_____	coherent incoherent	coherently incoherently
_____	conceive	conceivable inconceivable	conceivably inconceivably
_____	_____	inherent	inherently
presumption	presume	presumptuous	presumably

A. Complete the paragraph below with the target words from the Word Form Chart. Use the correct form and tense of each word.

Linguists study the origin, meaning, and use of languages. Recently, some

linguists have ___*presumed*___ that a new "World English" is developing.

(1. assumed)

However, others think that it is _____ that one new type of English

(2. unimaginable)

could develop because there are _____ linguistic and cultural

(3. basic part of something)

differences related to how people speak English around the world.

Nonetheless, there is a movement to _____ grammar rules to represent

(4. revise)

all the ways English is spoken worldwide. Some experts insist that it is

_____ to think that linguists can influence how a language is used, as

(5. overly confident)

language cannot be artificially created. At this point, there is no _____

(6. clear)

evidence to prove the existence of a new World English.

A *thesis* is (a) "a long piece of writing completed by a student as part of a degree, based on [the student's own] research."

  Roger completed his **thesis** *on geological instruments in three months.*

A *thesis* may also be (b) "a statement or opinion that is discussed in a logical way and presented with evidence in order to prove that it is true."

  Sarah's **thesis** *statement was unrelated to her paper.*

CORPUS

B. Write *a* or *b* to show which sense of *thesis* is used in each sentence.

_a_ 1. After completing my doctoral thesis, I got a job as an assistant professor.

____ 2. Many master's degree programs require students to complete a thesis in order to graduate.

____ 3. The essay had a thesis, but it was not supported by any details or information.

____ 4. The paper was well written and had a clear thesis statement.

C. *Instrinsic* means "belonging to or part of the real nature of something or someone." *Extrinsic* means "coming from or existing outside of something." Work with a partner to complete the chart.

Intrinsic rewards for workers or students	Extrinsic rewards for workers or students
1. *ability to choose*	1. *pay*
2. *confidence*	2. *high grades*
3.	3.
4.	4.
5.	5.

D. *Conceivable* is an adjective that describes something "that you can imagine or believe." Write whether the statements below are *C* (conceivable) or *I* (inconceivable). Add your own idea to the list. Discuss your answers with a partner. Which do you think will happen in the next 50 years?

____ 1. Robots will do all household work.

____ 2. Humans will travel to other worlds.

____ 3. People will live to be 150 years of age.

____ 4. People will fly to work instead of driving.

____ 5. _____

E. *Amend* means "to change a law, document, or statement in order to correct a mistake or to improve it." With a partner, discuss documents a person might amend at the following places.

1. at a company office *an invoice, a memo, a sales report*

2. at a school

3. in a government office

4. at a bank or credit union

About the Topic

Linguistics is the study of how languages are structured and how they develop. Two theories studied in linguistics are *Universalism* and *Relativism*. *Universalism* means "true or right at all times and places." *Relativism* is a "belief that something people think is true may not always be valid and that truth should be judged based on specific cirumstances."

Before You Listen

Read these questions. Discuss your answers in a small group.

1. What is the most difficult language to learn?

2. Do you think speaking a language is entirely learned, or is it an inherent ability that people are born with?

3. Do different languages have different ways of expressing thoughts and feelings? Explain your answer.

Listen

Read the Listen for Main Ideas activity below. Go online to listen to a lecture about the sociology of language. A professor discusses some of the interesting debates in the field.

Listen for Main Ideas

Mark each sentence as *T* (true) or *F* (false). Work with a partner. Restate false sentences to make them correct.

____ 1. Linguistic Relativism says that the language we speak affects how we think and how we view the world.

____ 2. Linguistic Universalism says that all humans see the world in similar ways.

____ 3. According to one study, German and Spanish speakers think about and experience a bridge in the same way.

____ 4. The professor supports Linguistic Universalism.

NOTE-TAKING SKILL Telegraphic Language

LEARN

During a lecture, you should take notes on main ideas, supporting information, and keywords. Do not try to write down every word you hear. It takes too much time, and you may lose track of what the lecturer is saying.

To follow the lecture and take good notes, use short forms of words when you write the information that you hear. Remember, there is no one correct way to write notes. Develop a system that works well for you.

Use Telegraphic Language: In your notes, you can ignore grammar rules and write only keywords and phrases. You can also omit vowels from words to write information faster.

Use Abbreviations and Symbols: Use the abbreviations and symbols in the chart on page 77 to represent words from a lecture or speech as you write your notes. Use numbers to stand for numerical values.

Word	Abbreviation	Word	Symbol
with, without	w/, w/o	equal / not equal	= ≠
because	b/c	increase / decrease	< >
and so on	etc.	causes / becomes	→
for example	e.g.	and	+
before	b4	important	*
question, answer	Q, A	not understand	?

APPLY

A. To the chart above, add a symbol and an abbreviation that you like to use when taking notes. Compare abbreviations and symbols with a partner.

B. Listen to the first part of the lecture again. Take notes on the main idea and important details, using telegraphic language, abbreviations, and symbols. Compare your notes with a partner.

Title: Sociology of Language

I. Language → born w/ or learned?
*   A. brain functions → _____*
*   B. debated issue*

II. Language affects thinking
*   A. Ling Relativism = _____*
*   B. Ling Universalism = _____*

C. Go online to listen to another part of the lecture. As you listen, continue to take notes using telegraphic language, symbols, and abbreviations.

III. Gender in language w/ bridge
*   A. Germ spkrs → br. feminine e.g., _____*
*   B. Span spkrs → br. masculine e.g., _____*

IV. Australian study
*   Kuuk Thaayorre spkrs _____*

V. Another study _____
*   _____*

D. Work with a partner. Summarize the two parts of the lecture, using your notes. One person should summarize part B, the other person, part C.

Vocabulary Activities

A. Cross out the word or phrase in parentheses that has a different meaning from the others. Use a dictionary to help you understand new words.

1. The company integrated all their computer systems (~~despite allowing~~ / to allow / thereby allowing / and, by these means, allowing) everyone to access their information more easily.

2. Understanding social (*norms* / *exchanges* / *behaviors* / *standards*) can provide insight into a cultural group.

3. The CEO made a(n) (*arbitrary* / *quick* / *uninformed* / *random*) decision to cancel the project.

4. The village has (*funded* / *retained* / *kept* / *maintained*) the custom for many years.

5. The official's speech contained many (*unclear* / *dramatic* / *ambiguous* / *vague*) statements that her listeners did not understand.

6. The students (*advanced* / *furthered* / *promoted* / *implemented*) health education by distributing related informational brochures to others.

B. For the target word below, match the dictionary definitions on the left with the example sentences on the right.

promote

Definitions

_b_ 1. to help something to happen or develop

___ 2. to help sell a product or service or make it more popular

___ 3. to move someone to a higher rank or more senior job

Example Sentences

a. The phone company is promoting their new monthly rates to attract customers.

b. The government created a new agency to promote economic growth in the province.

c. Sue was promoted to the position of manager last week.

Immigrate means "to come and live permanently in a country after leaving your own." *Immigrate* is frequently used with the preposition *to*. An *immigrant* is "a person who has come to live permanently in a country that is not their own."

My family and I **immigrated** to Germany when I was young.

In Toronto, **immigrants** account for nearly half of the city's population.

The words *immigrate* and *emigrate* are often confused. The word *emigrate* means "to leave your own country to go and live permanently in another country." *Emigrate* is frequently used with the preposition *from*.

My family and I **emigrated from** Korea.

CORPUS

C. Use the correct form of *immigrate* once in each sentence below.

1. Many people have ___immigrated___ to Australia in recent years.

2. There are _____ from _____ living in _____.

3. When you pass through _____ at the airport, you need a _____.

4. _____ has a large _____ population.

5. Some people have emigrated from _____ and _____ to France.

Ambiguous means "not clearly stated or defined" or "can be understood in more than one way."

> The role of the company president's brother is **ambiguous**. Seriously, no one is sure what his job is!

> The politician's explanation was so **ambiguous**, no one understood what his position was.

Unambiguous means "clear in meaning" or "can only be understood in one way."

> The politician's statement was **unambiguous**; she clearly said that she fully supported the construction of a new soccer stadium.

 CORPUS

D. Write whether each statement is *A* (ambiguous) or *U* (unambiguous). If a statement is ambiguous, describe different meanings that it may have.

___A__ 1. The kid hit the woman with the bag. *Did the kid use the bag to hit the woman? Or, did the kid hit the woman who was holding the bag?*

_____ 2. John saw Sam on the street, so he went with him to his home for lunch.

_____ 3. The sign stated that photography was not allowed anywhere in the museum.

_____ 4. The boss really likes the project, but he's not sure if it is a good one.

_____ 5. The study showed that 200 people in the town speak Farsi.

E. Complete the sentences below for *retain*. Use each word from the box once.

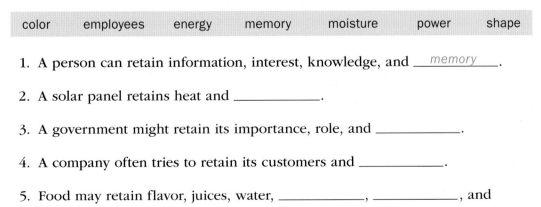

color	employees	energy	memory	moisture	power	shape

1. A person can retain information, interest, knowledge, and ___memory___.

2. A solar panel retains heat and _____.

3. A government might retain its importance, role, and _____.

4. A company often tries to retain its customers and _____.

5. Food may retain flavor, juices, water, _____, _____, and _____.

About the Topic

An *academic study* is a research project that tries to answer a specific question. Academic studies often collect data from observations, surveys, and other evidence to answer the specific question. Academic journals often publish the results of these studies.

Before You Watch

Read the questions below. Discuss your answers in a small group.

1. What do you do to maintain your health?

2. What is the most important factor in leading a happy life? Money? Family? Career?

3. What is the most important factor in leading a long life?

🕜 Watch

Read the Listen for Main Ideas activity below. Go online to watch a student summarize research on Blue Zones around the world. The research provides insight into the secrets behind living a long and happy life.

🕜 Listen for Main Ideas

Read the questions about the video. Work with a partner to choose the best answer.

1. What is a Blue Zone?

   a. a place where people live long lives

   b. a place with large numbers of immigrants

   c. a place where people can get excellent health care

2. In the study, what was one characteristic all Blue Zones shared?

   a. participation in professional sports

   b. no one smokes

   c. lots of physical activity

3. What kinds of food do people in Blue Zones mainly eat?

   a. They eat mostly fish.

   b. They eat fruit every day.

   c. They mostly eat a plant-based diet.

4. According to the presenter, why is this research important for everyone?

   a. The habits in the Blue Zone can be applied to every culture.

   b. We can learn cooking techniques from the Blue Zones.

   c. Governments need to learn how to develop Blue Zones.

I. Introduction	Research Topic: Blue Zones
	Researchers: Gianni Pes and Michel Poulainin
	Year Published: 2004
	Research Question: Why certain groups live _____? What promotes good health?
	Importance of Research Question: help _____
II. Body	Research Methods: collect data _____ studied Blue Zones → find _____
	Results: found _____ secret to long life = 5 _____ _____
III. Conclusion	Implications of Results: _____ _____
	Presenter's Opinion / Suggestion: _____ _____

APPLY

A. Work with a partner. Look at the notes above. Discuss some things that you remember about the student's summary.

B. Watch the video again. Add your own thoughts to the notes.

C. Compare your notes with a partner.

D. Working with your partner, use your notes to summarize the research in your own words.

LEARN

Use chunking, pausing, and intonation to help listeners process information.

A. Use chunking to list items in a series. Pause and use rising intonation at the end of each item. Signal the end of your list with falling intonation. Go online to listen.

Words	I've been to Spain, | Greece, | Italy, | and Jamaica.
Phrases	I'd like a double cheeseburger, | a large order of fries, | and a small Coke.
Clauses	I'd like to know where you went, | how long you were there, | and who you went with.
Independent clauses	I can sing, | I can play the guitar, | and I can dance.

B. Use chunking and pausing to divide explanatory speech into manageable units. Use rising intonation to signal there is more to come and falling intonation when you are finished. Go online to listen.

My first name's Jennifer: My last name's Tomlinson:
\| That's J-E-N \| N-I-F \| E-R.   \| T-O-M \| L-I-N \| S-O-N.

APPLY

A. Go online to listen to a woman giving personal information. Notice her chunking, pausing, and intonation. Draw in pause marks (\|) and intonation arrows.

1. My middle name's Katherine. \| You spell it \| k as in kite \| a as in alpha \| t as in tango \| h as in hotel \| e as in echo \| r as in Romeo \| i as in India \| n as in November \| and e as in echo.

2. My phone number's 2 1 3 5 5 5 9 8 9 7.

3. My email address is JENTOM25 at yahoo dot com. That's J–E–N–T–O–M 2 5 at yahoo dot com.

4. Visit me on the web at www dot me dot com forward slash Jen, that's j-e-n, Tomlinson.

5. Use my User ID when you log in. It's jkt25, that's j–k–t–2–5.

6. The password's a bit tricky. It's xq*E_257#AH-3.

B. Work with a group. Practice saying and hearing important words and numbers. Speakers: Use chunking, pausing, and intonation to guide your listeners. Listeners: Write what you hear and check your comprehension.

I live on Columbus Street. That's C-O | L-U-M | B-U-S.

C. With a partner, share some of your favorites, using topics from the chart below. Answer with a list of at least three items. Your partner should write your answers, and mark them for pausing and intonation. You will do the same for your partner's answers.

A. What are your favorite ice cream flavors?

B. Mango, | raspberry sorbet, | and chocolate mint chip.

What are your favorite ...	
foods?	English words?
sports?	songs in English?
movies?	subjects in school?
luxury cars?	leisure time activities?
vacation spots?	forms of entertainment?
cities in the world?	things to do on a Sunday?

End of Unit Task

In this unit, you learned about ways to take notes using abbreviations, symbols, and telegraphic language. You also learned how to summarize academic research. Review these skills by developing a summary with a small group. (If possible, work in a group of three.)

A. What are some interesting research projects or studies that you have heard or read about recently?

_____

_____

_____

B. Write notes about your research topic. If needed, use the Internet or a library to look up more information for your summary.

I. Introduction	Research Topic:	
	Researchers:	Year Published:
	Research Question:	
	Importance of Research Question:	

II. Body	Research Methods:
	Results:
III. Conclusion	Implications:
	Presenter's Opinion / Suggestion:

C. Divide the summary into three parts and practice presenting your summary.

D. Share your summary with another group. As you listen to the other group's summary, take notes on one part of the summary, using abbreviations, symbols, and telegraphic language. Be sure to divide the three parts among the three members of your group.

E. For the part that you took notes on, summarize the other group's presentation.

Self-Assessment		
Yes	**No**	
☐	☐	I took notes using abbreviations, symbols, and telegraphic language.
☐	☐	I successfully summarized academic research.
☐	☐	I listened to and summarized one part of a presentation.
☐	☐	I successfully used chunking, pausing, and intonation when speaking.
☐	☐	I can correctly use the target vocabulary words from the unit.

Discussion Questions

With a partner or in a small group, discuss the following questions.

1. Sociology is the scientific study of the nature and development of society and social behavior. What aspects of sociology are most interesting to you?

2. What is the best way to study human behavior: through surveys, observations, or other methods?

3. Why do humans create and organize governments and other institutions?

UNIT 8

Building an Idea

GOOD IDEA

In this unit, you will

> learn about entrepreneurship and operating a small business.

> increase your understanding of the target academic words for this unit.

LISTENING AND SPEAKING SKILLS

> The Cornell Note-Taking Method
> Supporting an Opinion
> **PRONUNCIATION** Chunking and Pausing for Clarity

Self-Assessment

Think about how well you know each target word, and check (✓) the appropriate column. I have...

TARGET WORDS	never seen this word before.	heard or seen the word but am not sure what it means.	heard or seen the word and understand what it means.	used the word confidently in *either* speaking or writing.
AWL				
administrate				
🔑 assure				
clause				
compensate				
complement				
confer				
confine				
🔑 definite				
🔑 derive				
entity				
🔑 estate				
🔑 occupy				
qualitative				
subsidy				

🔑 Oxford 3000™ keywords

Vocabulary Activities

Word Form Chart			
Noun	**Verb**	**Adjective**	**Adverb**
assurance	assure	assured	assuredly
compensation	compensate	compensatory	_____
complement	complement	complementary	_____
conference	confer	_____	_____
derivation derivative	derive	derived	_____
_____	_____	qualitative	qualitatively

A. Complete the paragraph below with the target words from the Word Form Chart. Use the correct form and tense of each word. Use the words in parentheses to help you. Some words may be used more than once.

The university is looking for business majors to participate in a ___qualitative___
(1. related to interpretations)

research study. This research project seeks to identify key technical skills

that _____ business school requirements and coursework. Students
(2. add to and improve)

are _____ that for participating in the study, they will receive
(3. guaranteed)

_____ of $50. Additionally, students are _____ that their names
(4. payment)   (5. promised)

and identities will not be used in any way. Conclusions _____ from
(6. formed from)

the study will be presented at three academic _____ next year.
(7. official meetings)

Derive means "to come or develop from something." It describes something that literally has its origin in something else.

> The new medication is **derived** from a common wildflower.

Derive also means "to get something (usually abstract) from something else." It usually refers to something good or positive.

> I **derive** great pleasure from hearing birds sing in the morning.

CORPUS

B. Draw an arrow pointing to the thing that is *derived*. Write whether the derivation is *L* (literal) or *A* (abstract).

_A_ 1. joy ← travel

___ 2. ancient texts ___ knowledge

___ 3. satisfaction ___ gardening

___ 4. chocolate ___ cocoa beans

___ 5. petroleum ___ gasoline

Definite means "certain; unlikely to change." The adverb is *definitely*.

> Could you give me a **definite** answer by tomorrow? I need to know if you are going.

> I am **definitely** interested in joining the basketball team.

Definitive means "final; unable to be changed" or "the best of its kind and almost impossible to improve."

> There won't be a **definitive** schedule until the committee decides which classes will be offered.

> Gildo wrote a **definitive** guide to teaching written English as a foreign language.

CORPUS

C. Fill in the blanks. Use *definite, definitely,* or *definitive*. Some statements may have more than one possible answer.

1. The newest edition was a ___definitive___ translation of the novel. It was excellent.

2. You should _____ ask someone how to do it before you try it yourself.

3. They couldn't give a _____ answer.

4. We have considered the plans, but nothing is _____ yet.

D. *Qualitative information* is based on interpretations and descriptions of something. *Quantitative information* is based on amounts and numbers. Write *QL* (qualitative) or *QN* (quantitative) to identify the type of information each sentence describes.

_QN_ 1. The research showed that 20 percent of all people support the program.

___ 2. Most of those questioned felt good about the study.

___ 3. We calculated and graphed all of the cases.

___ 4. The situation fits well with other situations that we have observed.

___ 5. The data showed that the event occurred 300 times last year.

E. *Complement* means "to add to something in a way that improves it or makes it more attractive." Complete the sentences below with your own ideas.

1. Rice and _____beans_____ complement each other nutritionally.

2. _____ complements a living room set quite nicely.

3. Nothing complements a suit as well as _____.

About the Topic

An entrepreneur is a person who tries to earn money by starting a business. If an entrepreneur has an idea for a product, he / she will often build a prototype. A prototype is the first design of something from which other forms are copied.

Before You Watch

Read the following questions. Discuss your answers in a small group.

1. Describe the features of your ideal work environment.

2. If you have a good idea for a business, what steps would you take to implement it?

3. What kinds of businesses are the easiest to start? The most difficult?

Watch

Read the Listen for Main Ideas activity below. Go online to watch a presentation at a conference on entrepreneurship. At the conference each year, people discuss trends in entrepreneurship and examine related research.

Listen for Main Ideas

Read the questions about the video. Work with a partner to ask and answer these questions.

1. The speaker conducts research on ___.
    a. finance and accounting
    b. manufacturing methods
    c. entrepreneurialism

2. The speaker discusses ___.
    a. ways to turn ideas into products
    b. best business practices
    c. the best ideas for new products

3. Some entrepreneurs work with ___ to build their products.
    a. tradespeople
    b. large corporations
    c. small investors

4. Members of TechShop ___.
    a. receive memberships based on their work experience
    b. use machines and tools that can be found at any store
    c. pay a fee to use industrial-strength machinery

NOTE-TAKING SKILL   The Cornell Note-Taking Method

LEARN

The Cornell Method is a way to take notes. You start by dividing your paper into three sections as shown below. The three sections help you take notes in class, study what you wrote down, and remember what you heard. Read the instructions off to the right for the Cornell Method.

Section A

Section B

- What type of research does the speaker do?

- _____

- _____

- _____

- qualitative research = entrepreneurialism

- changed research → turning ideas into products

- tradespeople
- _____
- _____

- _____
- cheaper than established companies
- students' skills and _____

Take notes here. Compare your notes with a partner. Then add information.

Write questions here about the notes you took in Section B.

Section C

Here, write a summary of the notes from Section B.

APPLY

A. Go online to watch part of the video and complete Section B in the notes box above.

B. Compare your answers with a partner. Add any additional information you think might be important.

C. Write a question in Section A for each point in Section B. Work with a partner. Ask and answer each other's questions. Confirm or correct the information in Section B.

D. As a class, create a summary in Section C in the box above.

Vocabulary Activities

A. Complete the chart below by writing the correct forms of the target words in the numbered cells.

Word Form Chart			
Noun	**Verb**	**Adjective**	**Adverb**
1. *administration* 2.	administrate	3.	administratively
confines	4.	5.	_____
occupancy 6. 7.	occupy	8.	_____
subsidy	9.	_____	_____

B. Match the definitions on the left with the example sentences on the right.

occupation

Definitions

_b_ 1. a job or profession

____ 2. how you spend your time, especially when you're not working

____ 3. the act of living in or using a building, room, or piece of land

Example Sentences

a. The apartment will be ready for occupation next month.

b. Nursing is a great occupation that allows me to work with people on a daily basis.

c. Since retiring, my grandmother's main occupation has been playing golf.

estate

Definitions

____ 1. all of the property and money owned by someone

____ 2. a large area of land, usually in the countryside, owned by a family or person

Example Sentences

a. Some of the farming families in our area have a large estate to manage.

b. After he died, his estate went to his children.

C. Work with a partner. Discuss five different things that might be part of a person's estate.

_____ _____ _____ _____ _____

D. *Entity* refers to a unit of something much larger that also exists separately and has its own identity. Work with a partner to fill out the chart below.

Entity	Administrative units
1. a university	*academic departments, enrollment offices, student services*
2. a large multinational corporation	_____ _____
3. _____	_____ _____

administrate	clause	confine	entity	estate	subsidy

E. Complete the following paragraph with target words from the box above. Use the correct form and tense of each word. One word will be used twice.

As an independent contractor, my sales company is considered a small

business ___*entity*___, even though my office is in my home. When I'm not
          (1. unit)

traveling to meet with clients, I do all of my _____ work at home.
                                                (2. managerial)

However, in recent years, I have felt _____ by what I can do at home.
                                        (3. limited)

For example, if a customer wants to meet me, it is unprofessional to invite

him / her to my home. So, I have started to look into buying commercial

real _____ to establish an office. Fortunately, I came across a
      (4. property)

_____ in a local government document, stating that the government
  (5. phrase)

provides _____ to small business owners for the purchasing of
          (6. financial support)

real _____. This will help me expand my business.
      (7. land)

About the Topic

Crop rotation is the practice of growing different things on different parts of the land in different years. Crop rotation helps to maintain the health of the soil and to increase production. As a result, this practice allows farmers to earn greater revenues, or money received from a business.

Before You Listen

Read the following questions. Discuss your answers in a small group.

1. Which kinds of businesses earn large revenues in your country?

2. Would you rather work for a small company or a large company? Explain your answer.

3. What kinds of crops do farmers usually grow in your state?

Listen

Read the Listen for Main Ideas activity below. Go online to listen to a radio show where a small business owner talks about what it takes to make a business successful.

Listen for Main Ideas

Mark each sentence as *T* (true) or *F* (false). Work with a partner. Restate false sentences to make them correct.

_F_ 1. The business owner operates his own sales company. *He is a farmer.*

____ 2. According to him, organization and planning are important for successfully operating a business.

____ 3. Agricultural subsidies can help some farmers in a time of need.

____ 4. It is easy for farmers to leave the farm for long periods of time.

SPEAKING SKILL   Supporting an Opinion

LEARN

In a university class or professional setting, you may be asked to discuss or present your opinion on a topic. Giving only your opinion, however, is often not enough. You will probably be expected to provide support for your opinion.

For example, imagine someone says the following:

In my opinion, all new drivers should have to take a road test.

The speaker may support his / her statement with examples, statistics (i.e., numerical data), information from an expert, or personal experience.

Example	When new drivers take road tests, they learn a great deal about driving from instructors. This process improves safety.
Statistics	In countries without road tests, there are higher rates of accidents among new drivers.

Expert opinion	Several academic studies have shown that road tests increase safety.
Personal experience	When I was young, I received my license without a road test, and I did not feel prepared to drive. I believe a road test would have helped me.

APPLY

A. Go online to listen to the audio again. Fill in the middle Support column.

Opinion	Support	Type of support
Yes, to a large extent, I believe that I'm a business owner.	• $300,000 in revenue • *finances req admin work*	Example Personal experience
In my view, the most important things are organization and planning.	• farmers plan → 5–10 years in advance • _____	_____ Personal experience
I think subsidies can be beneficial for some people.	• _____ • _____	_____

B. Work with a partner. Compare and revise the notes that you wrote in activity A.

C. Looking at the different types of support in the chart on pages 92–93, label each type of support in the third column.

D. What is your opinion on violent video games?

1. Give your opinion.

2. Provide two different types of support for your opinion.

3. Share your opinion with the class.

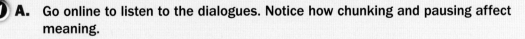

PRONUNCIATION SKILL | Chunking and Pausing for Clarity

LEARN

Chunking and pausing are the "punctuation marks" of spoken English. Use them to create meaning by dividing your words into groups.

A. Go online to listen to the dialogues. Notice how chunking and pausing affect meaning.

Teacher:	What's (2 x 6) + 2? (What's two times six | plus two?)	Teacher:	What's 2 x (6 + 2)? (What's two | times six plus two?)
Student:	Fourteen.	Student:	Sixteen.

A:	How many jobs do you have?	A:	I've been self-employed for ten years.
B:	I have two.	B:	I have, | too.

Cashier:	Debit or credit?	Cashier:	Debit | or credit?
Customer:	Yes.	Customer:	Debit.

APPLY

A. Go online to listen. You will hear phrase *a* or *b*. Notice the chunking. Then match the meaning with one of the phrases on the right.

1. (a.) We had chocolate cake and ice cream.	✓ chocolate cake | ice cream
b. We had chocolate, cake, and ice cream.	___ chocolate | cake | ice cream
2. a. Where's the phone bill?	___ the phone bill
b. Where's the phone, Bill?	___ the phone | Bill
3. a. He interviewed the criminals, the judge, and the police.	___ the criminals | the judge | the police
b. He interviewed the criminals: the judge and the police.	___ the criminals | the judge and the police
4. a. She's into video games and electronic gadgets.	___ video games | electronic gadgets
b. She's into video, games, and electronic gadgets.	___ video | games | electronic gadgets

B. Go online to listen to the statements. Check (✓) the corresponding meaning.

___ 1. Ann is an outstanding scholar.

___ The professor is an outstanding scholar.

___ 2. Only Tony speaks English.

___ Both Tony and Tom speak English.

C. Read each pair of statements in Column A. Then go online to listen to them. Circle the sentence you hear.

Column A	Column B
1. Why don't you ask Lee? (Why don't you ask, Lee?)	___ I apologize. I didn't mean to annoy you.
2. I'm afraid I can't do it. I'm afraid. I can't do it.	___ That's too bad. We were really looking forward to seeing you.
3. I don't think I know. I don't think. I know.	___ No problem. I'll ask someone else.

4. Don't stop! Don't! Stop!	___1___ I'm too embarrassed.
5. I'm sorry I can't make it. I'm sorry. I can't make it.	_____ Yes, please.
6. Coffee or tea? Coffee? Or tea?	_____ I'm sorry I doubted you!

D. Match the appropriate responses in Column B to the statements you circled in Column A by inserting the corresponding problem number.

E. Work with a partner. Look at the statements that you did not circle in Apply, activity C. Write possible responses. Practice the new dialogues.

> *A: Why don't you ask Lee?*
> *B: Because I don't think he knows.*

End of Unit Task

In this unit, you learned how to take notes using the Cornell Method. You also learned how to support your opinions. Practice both of these skills by creating a presentation with a partner.

A. Choose a company that you are familiar with or that you are interested in.

B. Create a presentation about the company you chose in activity A. Answer the following questions to help you develop your presentation.

 I. Introduction

What does the company do? _____

What does it produce? _____

Where does it operate? _____

What size is it? _____

 II. Your Opinion on the Strengths of the Company

What does the company do well? _____

How is the quality of its products? _____

How successful is the company? _____

III. Your Opinion on Its Weaknesses

In what ways is the company weak? _____

How is the quality of its products? _____

What could the company do better? _____

IV. Conclusion

What is your prediction with respect to the future of the company?

_____

C. With your partner, revise your presentation. Make sure that you support your statements and opinions about the company that you selected with examples, statistics, expert opinions, and personal experience.

D. Work with another pair of students. Take turns sharing your presentations with each other. As you listen, take notes on the other presentation in Section B.

E. Continue working with the other pair, and complete Section A. Take turns asking each other at least two questions from your notes.

F. Write a summary of the other group's presentation in Section C. Take turns sharing summaries.

Section A	Section B
Section C	

Take notes here. Compare your notes with a partner. Then add information.

Write questions here about the notes you took in Section B.

Here, write a summary of the notes from Section B.

Self-Assessment		
Yes	**No**	
☐	☐	I used the Cornell Method to take notes.
☐	☐	I supported my opinion by using examples, statistics, an expert's opinion, and personal experience.
☐	☐	I successfully created a presentation about a company.
☐	☐	I use chunking and pausing to make my meaning clear when speaking.
☐	☐	I can correctly use the target vocabulary words from the unit.

Discussion Questions

With a partner or in a small group, discuss the following questions.

1. Which aspect of business interests you most: finance, accounting, marketing, administration, or a different one?

2. What is the main reason why some businesses succeed and others fail?

UNIT 9

High-Performance Machines

In this unit, you will

> learn about the roles of robots and computers in medicine.
> increase your understanding of the target academic words for this unit.

LISTENING AND SPEAKING SKILLS

> Facts and Opinions
> Polite Requests and Interruptions
> **PRONUNCIATION** New Information and Special Emphasis

Self-Assessment

Think about how well you know each target word, and check (✓) the appropriate column. I have…

TARGET WORDS	never seen this word before.	heard or seen the word but am not sure what it means.	heard or seen the word and understand what it means.	used the word confidently in *either* speaking or writing.
AWL				
🔑 behalf				
🔑 bond				
compile				
dimension				
exploit				
finite				
incorporate				
🔑 index				
🔑 injure				
inspect				
offset				
protocol				
undergo				
welfare				

🔑 Oxford 3000™ keywords

Vocabulary Activities

Finite means "having a definite limit or fixed size."

> Some physicists believe that the universe is **finite**, but they do not claim to know its exact limits.

Infinite means "without limits; without end," or "very great and impossible to measure." It is often used figuratively. The adverb is *infinitely*.

> This new technology has **infinite** potential to improve health.

> The latest software allows the robot to do an **infinite** number of calculations.

> Our department is **infinitely** more efficient than it was before we implemented the new software.

CORPUS

A. Complete the following sentences with the correct form of either *finite* or *infinite*.

1. Most animals have a(n) _____finite_____ lifespan.

2. The computer's memory seems to contain a(n) _____ amount of data.

3. The number of new computer applications seems to be increasing _____ .

4. Given her other responsibilities, the doctor has a(n) _____ amount of time available for training.

5. The specific descriptions of the suspect seem to match a(n) _____ number of people.

6. I was _____ more confident about my résumé after my professor revised it.

Word Form Chart			
Noun	**Verb**	**Adjective**	**Adverb**
compilation	compile	_____	_____
dimension	_____	dimensional multidimensional	_____
exploit exploitation	exploit	_____	_____
_____	_____	finitc infinite	infinitely
index	index	_____	_____
offset	offset	_____	_____

B. Complete the paragraph on page 99 with the target words from the Word Form Chart above. Use the correct form and tense of each word.

Automation is the use of automatic equipment, such as robots and computers, to do jobs or tasks. Increasingly, humans are ___*exploiting*___ robot technology
(1. developing or using)
to improve efficiency. Because of their _____ capabilities, robots can
(2. having many aspects)
be used in an almost _____ number of industrial tasks. For example,
(3. uncountable)
in the workplace, automated processes are highly productive because
computers can _____ , store, and _____ large amounts of
(4. gather)　　　　　　　(5. organize)
data very quickly. In fact, some people wonder whether gains in economic
efficiency will be _____ by job losses caused by increased automation.
(6. balanced)

Index has several meanings:

a. a list of names or topics that are referred to in a book, usually arranged at the end of the book

b. a system that shows the level of prices and pay

c. a sign or a measure that something else can be judged by

CORPUS

C. Using the information from above, write the letter that matches the meaning of *index* used in each sentence below.

_a_ 1. You can determine which famous historical figures are discussed by checking the index.

____ 2. The consumer quality index assesses the quality of a wide range of products.

____ 3. The items in the index are presented in alphabetical order.

____ 4. The index that tracks the stock market increased by three percent.

Behalf means "in order to help someone." It is often used in the phrases *on behalf of* and *on (someone's) behalf.*

The volunteers worked **on behalf of** the children.

The manager spoke **on** the team's **behalf.**

Behalf also means "as a representative of someone or instead of them."

On behalf of the company, I would like to express our sincerest thanks.

CORPUS

D. Choose the best phrase on the right to complete each sentence on the left.

_b_ 1. The nurse spoke on behalf of　　a. the team.

____ 2. The coach thanked the fans on behalf of　　b. the patient.

____ 3. The spokesperson gave a speech on behalf of　　c. the administration.

About the Topic

Emissions are gases that are sent out into the air. Electric cars do not directly burn fuels that give off emissions. Instead, they run on batteries that a person can recharge by using electricity. Because electric cars are newer than traditional automobiles, experts often pay particular attention to their performance and reliability ratings.

Before You Listen

Read these questions. Discuss your answers in a small group.

1. What are some interesting uses of robots in recent years?
2. What are some benefits of driving an electric car?
3. What are some disadvantages of driving an electric car?

Listen

Read the Listen for Main Ideas activity below. Go online to listen to an interview at a car company. The employee at the automotive plant shares information on electric-powered cars and automation.

Listen for Main Ideas

Mark each sentence as *T* (true) or *F* (false). Work with a partner. Restate false sentences to make them correct.

___T___ 1. The Model V is an electric-powered car.

_____ 2. Consumer reports have given the Model V low ratings.

_____ 3. According to the interview, the car has many functions.

_____ 4. Robots only perform very basic tasks at the Mata factory.

LISTENING SKILL   Facts and Opinions

LEARN

Distinguishing between a fact and an opinion can be difficult. Speakers often state facts using statistics, names, dates, places, or events.

> *Last year, housing prices rose by five percent.*

> *The event took place in Detroit in 1984.*

An opinion expresses someone's feelings, thoughts, or judgments about something. Remember that sometimes facts are used to support an opinion. Notice that the second part of the following sentence is an opinion.

> *We have been building robots for 50 years, and we do an excellent job.*

Here are some things to listen for to help you determine whether something is an opinion.

Superlative statements	Adverbs and adjectives	Doubt and probability
Our floor design is the most elegant one in the city. We carry the finest fruits and vegetables. This is the worst proposal that I have ever seen.	We have received a considerable amount of support. They are hardworking. We received insufficient funding for the project.	It might be a good idea. We should probably delay the project. The athlete has some potential.

APPLY

A. Work with a partner. Look at the statements. Write whether each is an opinion (*O*) or a fact (*F*). For the opinion sentences, underline the words or phrases that show it's an opinion.

_F_ 1. The company was sold last week.

___ 2. This workbook should help students develop their skills.

___ 3. An incredibly large number of people voted for the policy.

___ 4. Vandana Shiva was born in 1952.

___ 5. Gordon was the most capable scientist there.

B. Go online to listen to part of the audio again. First, complete each sentence. Then indicate whether each one is an opinion (*O*) or a fact (*F*).

_O_ 1. Well, to start, it's _____the finest_____ sedan in the world.

___ 2. The Model V is an electric car that produces _____ CO_2 gas.

___ 3. We can't _____ all of our resources and hope that they'll never run out.

___ 4. Electric _____, and we're proving it here.

___ 5. The Model V is not only a green car, but also _____ high-performance vehicle.

___ 6. This car goes from _____ in less than five seconds.

___ 7. It has a 17-inch _____.

___ 8. And you can select a _____ interior with elegant leather trim. And all versions have spacious, _____ seating.

C. Discuss your opinion of the following question in a small group: *What is the best car for a young professional to drive?* Support your opinion with facts.

Vocabulary Activities

A. Cross out the word or phrase in parentheses that has a different meaning from the others. Use a dictionary to help you understand new words.

1. The new child-protection law promotes the (*well-being / success / health and safety / welfare*) of children.

2. The athlete (*punished / wounded / injured / hurt*) his ankle during the game.

3. Researchers noted the strong (*bonds / connections / links / limits*) among family members in the study.

4. The company (*combined / merged / incorporated / designed*) the new software into its existing system.

5. The officials follow standard (*procedures / incentives / protocols / established methods*) when processing a tourist visa.

6. The security guards (*recognized / inspected / checked / examined*) the passengers' baggage as they passed through the gates.

7. Since I was last here, the city has (*avoided / undergone / gone through / experienced*) much change.

B. Some words have multiple meanings. For the target word below, match the dictionary definitions on the left with the example sentences on the right.

bond

Definitions

_b_ 1. something that forms a connection between people or groups

___ 2. an agreement by a government or a company to pay you interest on money that you have lent

___ 3. anything that stops you from being free to do what you want

___ 4. the way in which two things are joined together

Example Sentences

a. This glue will create a strong bond between any two surfaces.

b. The two boys share a special bond. They are very good friends.

c. The government bond pays dividends.

d. I want to be released from the bonds of being a graduate student.

Undergo means "to experience something, especially a change or something unpleasant."

*The downtown area has **undergone** a complete transformation. It looks totally different than it did several years ago.*

CORPUS

C. Complete the following sentences with your own opinions. Discuss your answers with a partner.

1. _____ is a city that has undergone a lot of change in recent years.

2. _____ is a place that has undergone very little change over time.

3. _____ is a person who has undergone a great deal of change.

4. _____ has undergone a total transformation.

D. *Protocol* refers to a system of fixed rules and formal behavior. Rank the following situations in response to the question: *How important is it for the following people to follow standard protocol?* Use a scale of 1 to 5, where 1 = most important and 5 = least important. Discuss your rankings with a partner.

____ 1. a teacher when deciding students' grades

____ 2. a company when deciding to hire someone

____ 3. a doctor when doing a medical check-up

____ 4. a researcher when doing an academic study

____ 5. a builder when constructing the foundation of a building

E. Match the following nouns with their collocations.

Collocations

_e_ 1. suffer, cause, prevent

____ 2. form, develop, strengthen

____ 3. issue, downgrade, buy

____ 4. conduct, undergo, pass

____ 5. follow, approve, sign

Nouns

a. an investment bond

b. an inspection

c. a protocol

d. a bond of friendship

e. an injury

About the Topic

The sun is a major source of ultraviolet light on Earth. Humans cannot see ultraviolet light directly with our eyes, but we do use it. Ultraviolet light is sometimes used to kill bacteria and germs that cause infections, or illnesses caused by bacteria.

Before You Watch

Read the following questions. Discuss your answers in a small group.

1. How can robots improve medicine and health services?
2. What should the primary focus of a country's health care system be?
3. What are the characteristics of a good doctor?

🔊 Watch

Read the Listen for Main Ideas activity below. Go online to watch a student describe her research project. She discusses some of the ways that robots are being used in medicine.

🔊 Listen for Main Ideas

Read the questions about the video. Work with a partner to ask and answer these questions.

1. What is the future outlook for the use of robots in medicine?
   a. The use of robots is expected to increase in medicine.
   b. Robots will be used only for basic patient services.
   c. Robots may not be used to communicate with patients.

2. What do remote-presence robots do?
   a. They visit people's homes in emergencies.
   b. They detect problems before a doctor can.
   c. They allow a doctor to visit patients even if the doctor is not at the hospital.

3. Why are robots able to clean better than humans can?
   a. They use more advanced cleaners.
   b. They use ultraviolet light.
   c. They have more cleaning tools.

4. How well have surgical robots performed for doctors who have used them?
   a. Surgical robots have performed well.
   b. Surgical robots have not performed well.
   c. We do not have accurate data yet.

SPEAKING SKILL · Polite Requests and Interruptions

LEARN

When you make a polite request, you ask for something formally. Being able to make polite requests is important in academic and professional settings because it conveys a serious and professional attitude.

Polite requests
<u>If you have a moment,</u> could you please explain more about your research methods?
<u>If possible, could you</u> explain more about your research methods?
<u>Would you be able to</u> tell us more about your research methods?
<u>Could you perhaps</u> tell us more about your research methods?

When you interrupt someone, you start speaking before that person has completely finished. Interrupting is a difficult skill to develop because it can be considered impolite. Nonetheless, in a professional setting, you may need to interrupt someone. If you do interrupt someone, make sure you do so at an appropriate time and in a polite way.

When you might consider interrupting ...	When you might avoid interrupting ...
Group meeting	Class or professional presentation
Class discussion	Professor's lecture
Study session	
Discussion with a partner	

Polite interruptions
If I could just interject something, the data seem to indicate an increase.
I'd like to make a remark on that. The data seem to indicate an increase.
Sorry, I'd like to add something to what you just said. The data seem to indicate an increase.
If you don't mind, may I stop you for a moment? Where did you find the data?
I'm sorry to interrupt, but could you explain where you found the data?

APPLY

A. Work with a partner. Discuss different polite requests for the situations below.

1. You want to get information on rental options from a car company employee.

2. You want a presenter to explain what he / she said again.

3. You want to know more about the project your boss has assigned you.

B. Read the statements below. Then go online to watch part of the video again, and fill in the blanks.

1. ___Sorry to interrupt___ , but I was wondering …

2. _____ how the robots are able to move around the hospital?

3. Yes, _____ on that, actually.

4. _____ tell us whether or not doctors have commented on this potential problem?

5. If I _____ for a moment, I know that many cleaning companies have begun to incorporate robots …

C. Look at the statements in activity B. With a partner, discuss which ones are polite requests and which are polite interruptions.

LEARN

In spoken English, use stress to draw attention to *focus words*. A focus word is the most important idea in a chunk. Every English chunk has at least one focus word. It sounds stronger, longer, clearer, and usually higher than the other words in the phrase. Choosing focus words to highlight the main idea in a sentence is called *sentence focus*. Use this skill to introduce new information and signal special emphasis.

A. Go online to listen. The focus words written in pink below introduce a new topic in each sentence or phrase. Notice that this new information is usually the last content word (noun, main verb, adjective, adverb) in the chunk.

> The Model V electric car | causes 50 percent less CO_2. | So, when you're driving one of our cars, | you're helping | to offset CO_2 emissions. | Also, | don't forget: | Natural resources | are finite. | We can't continue | to exploit our resources | and hope | that they'll never run out. | Electric | is the future.

B. Listen to the above content again. Notice how repeated information is unstressed because it is no longer new. The combination of stress and unstress creates contrast between the focus words and the other words in the phrases.

APPLY

A. Go online to listen to the sentences. Circle the focus word in each chunk.

1. That's a great (question).
2. Robotics | is an extremely fascinating field.
3. There are thousands of robots | doing a wide variety of tasks | in hospitals.
4. Robots | can use | very sensitive GPS equipment.
5. Robots | are far better | at cleaning | than humans.

B. Go online to listen to five conversations. On a separate sheet of paper, write out the conversations. Chunk when necessary and underline the focus words. Compare your answers with a partner.

C. Practice the conversations in Apply, activity B with a partner. Create contrast by making focus words extra strong, extra long, extra high, and extra clear. Give significantly less stress to the other words in the sentences.

D. Work with another partner. Write two short conversations that contrast new and old information. Practice the conversations and teach them to another group.

> A: I ran into this **guy.**
> B: **What** guy?
> A: A guy from one of my **classes.**

*B: **Which** class?*

*A: My **physics** class.*

E. Practice the conversation below with your partner. Stretch out the words that add special emphasis. Then practice similar exchanges using the intensifying adverbs *so, totally, very, incredibly,* and *extremely.*

> *A: I'm r-e-a-l-l-y **tired**.*
>
> *B: **How** tired **are** you?*
>
> *A: I'm s-o-o-o **tired** that I could **sleep** for a **week**.*

End of Unit Task

In this unit, you learned how to listen for facts and opinions. You also learned about ways to interrupt politely and make polite requests. Review these skills by discussing a new technology with a partner.

Before beginning the tasks below, go online and find at least four facts about a new technology that is interesting to you. Then complete activity A.

A. Think of an interesting new technology. Write four different types of facts and three different types of opinions about the technology that you researched.

Fact statements	Opinion statements
1. (name, date)	1. (superlative)
2. (place, event)	2. (adverbs or adjective)
3. (statistic)	3. (doubt or probability)
4. (statistic)	

B. Work in a small group of three. Take turns discussing the facts and opinions about the technology that you chose. As you listen to your group members share their information, politely interrupt each speaker twice. Make sure that you use different phrases listed in the chart below. Check (✓) the phrases you used.

Polite ways to interrupt	(✓)
If I could just interject something, …	
I'd like to make a remark on that.	
Sorry, I'd like to add something to what you just said.	
If you don't mind, may I stop you for a moment?	
I'm sorry to interrupt, but where did you find the data?	

C. Write three different types of polite requests that you can use to get more information about the technology that your group discussed. As you write your polite requests, you may want to refer to page 104.

1. _____

2. _____

3. _____

D. As a class, choose someone (could be the instructor) to present a new technology or gadget. Use three polite interruptions and three polite requests.

1. As the person is presenting, raise your hands and use one of the phrases to interrupt politely. After interrupting, make a polite request for information about the technology that is being presented.

2. Take notes on the three polite interruptions and requests that are made.

3. After the presentation, discuss your notes as a class.

Polite interruptions	Polite requests
1.	1.
2.	2.
3.	3.

Self-Assessment		
Yes	**No**	
☐	☐	I was able to listen for different types of facts and opinions.
☐	☐	I interrupted a discussion in a polite manner.
☐	☐	I successfully used different phrases to make polite requests.
☐	☐	I can use stress to draw attention to focus words when speaking.
☐	☐	I can correctly use the target vocabulary words from the unit.

Discussion Questions

With a partner or in a small group, discuss the following questions.

1. What are some ways that robots may play a greater role in our lives in the future?

2. Despite future developments in technology, what kinds of tasks or jobs will humans always be able to do better than robots can?

3. Some scientists have predicted that technology will one day allow robots to think independently. Do you think this will be possible?

UNIT 10

A World Apart

In this unit, you will

> learn how language can shape how we experience the world.
> increase your understanding of the target academic words for this unit.

LISTENING AND SPEAKING SKILLS

> Synthesizing Information
> Deductive and Inductive Reasoning
> **PRONUNCIATION** Contrastive Stress in Sentences

Self-Assessment

Think about how well you know each target word, and check (✓) the appropriate column. I have...

TARGET WORDS	never seen this word before.	heard or seen the word but am not sure what it means.	heard or seen the word and understand what it means.	used the word confidently in *either* speaking or writing.
AWL				
append				
coincide				
concurrent				
🔑 core				
deduce				
denote				
deviate				
fluctuate				
forthcoming				
manipulate				
mediate				
sole				
terminate				
whereby				

🔑 Oxford 3000™ keywords

Vocabulary Activities

A. For each target word below, match the dictionary definitions on the left with the example sentences on the right.

forthcoming

Definitions

_a_ 1. going to happen very soon

___ 2. ready or made available when needed

___ 3. willing to give information about something

Example Sentences

a. New changes to the website are forthcoming.

b. Our boss is not very forthcoming about the company's latest plans.

c. Financial aid is not forthcoming, so I plan to get a job this semester.

coincide

Definitions

___ 1. to take place at the same time

___ 2. to be the same or very similar

___ 3. to meet or share the same space

Example Sentences

a. The two professors felt the same about the policy; for once their opinions coincided!

b. The new road coincides with the ancient one underneath it.

c. Fortunately, the dates of the conference and the cultural fair do not coincide.

Whereby means "by which" or "because of which." However, *whereas* is used to contrast two facts.

> *The company has implemented a new sales strategy **whereby** all customers are given a ten percent discount.*

> *The technical school has a two-year program, **whereas** the university offers a four-year degree.*

CORPUS

B. Complete the sentences using *whereby* or *whereas*.

1. Alasdair likes mysteries, ___whereas___ Paulo prefers history books.

2. The company developed a system _____ a person could learn a new language in three months.

3. The company has a new discount pass _____ tourists can visit any part of the country for one low price.

Deviate means "to do something in a different way from what is usual or expected."

*My grandparents always follow an itinerary on our family vacations—they don't like to **deviate** from their plans.*

CORPUS

C. Fill out the survey below. Discuss your answers with a partner.

1. During a vacation, a person should not *deviate* from his / her prearranged plans.

   agree | somewhat agree | somewhat disagree | disagree

2. When a manager gives a person instructions, sometimes it is OK to *deviate* from those instructions in order to get better results.

   agree | somewhat agree | somewhat disagree | disagree

3. It is OK to *deviate* from the truth if no one gets hurt.

   agree | somewhat agree | somewhat disagree | disagree

4. A person should not *deviate* from the norms of his / her workplace.

   agree | somewhat agree | somewhat disagree | disagree

D. To *append* means to add something to the end of a piece of writing. An *appendix* is a "section giving extra information at the end of a book or document." Work with a partner. Discuss three specific uses for an *appendix*.

1. *to include a chart for further information*

2. _____

3. _____

E. *Fluctuate* means "to change frequently in size, amount, or quality." With a partner, discuss how much you think the following items fluctuate. Write *1* for "a lot of fluctuation," *2* for "little fluctuation," or *3* for "no fluctuation."

____ 1. monthly rent for a specific apartment in the city

____ 2. the stock market

____ 3. the temperature in the summer

____ 4. a teacher's salary over his / her career

____ 5. your interest in world travel

F. *Sole* means "only" or "single." Match each statement on the left with the phrase on the right that best completes it.

_b_ 1. The scholarship money is solely for the purpose of   a. increasing sales.

____ 2. The company's sole focus is   b. paying tuition.

____ 3. Alex was not hired solely because of   c. a discounted price.

____ 4. The sole reason for buying the tickets three months in advance was to get   d. his lack of experience.

About the Topic

Ethnography is the study of the customs of individual people and cultures through close observation. Some researchers have lived in remote, or isolated, places to conduct an ethnographic study of a cultural group up close. Ethnographic studies can allow for detailed and insightful observations.

Before You Listen

Read the questions below. Discuss your answers in a small group.

1. What is the most remote place you have ever been to?
2. If you could go anywhere in the world, where would you go?
3. What cultural group would you be interested in studying?

Listen

Read the Listen for Main Ideas activity below. Go online to listen to a professor discuss her ethnographic study of Inuit people in Canada's Nunavut Territory.

Listen for Main Ideas

Choose the letter of the best answer to complete each sentence.

1. Nunavut has ___ .
   a. hot summers
   b. a moderate climate
   c. a cold climate

2. Nunavut covers ___ .
   a. a large area
   b. a small area
   c. an area the size of Spain

3. Traditional practices are ___ in Nunavut.
   a. no longer followed
   b. always followed
   c. followed in some cases

4. According to the speaker, Nunavut leaders are ___ .
   a. concerned with cultural preservation
   b. looking to establish an Inuit-centered university
   c. lacking transportation resources

5. The speaker ___ .
   a. had difficulty with the Inuit people
   b. enjoyed the experience
   c. also studied climate change

LEARN

When you listen to a lecture, in order to better understand and think critically about what you have heard, you can follow a three-step process. First, note key information and facts that you hear. Second, use the key information to identify the concepts that the speaker is talking about. Third, after you have recorded the key information and identified the concepts, synthesize the two by deciding what the information means or what your opinion of the information is.

APPLY

A. Go online to listen to part of the audio again. In the first column, record the key information that you hear.

Key information	Concepts
Nunavut temperature → _____	Commun & travel are challenges
Nunavut size = _____, communities are spread out	How can the govt improve connxn b/w towns
Travel b/w towns by _____	Challenges of living in cold climate
Traditional culture _____ _____	_____ _____
Education _____ _____ _____	_____ _____ _____

B. Work in a small group. Using the key information, think of at least one related concept for each set of information and write the concept in the right column in the chart in activity A. Share your answers with the class.

C. Continue working in your small group. Choose two of the concepts from the chart in activity A.

1. _____

2. _____

D. With your small group, synthesize the key information and related concepts that you chose.

1. What is their significance?

2. What is your opinion on them?

A. Complete the chart with the correct forms of the target words. If you need help, use a dictionary.

		Word Form Chart	
Noun	**Verb**	**Adjective**	**Adverb**
_____	_____	concurrent	1. *concurrently*
2.	deduce	_____	_____
3.	4.	manipulative	_____
5.	mediate	_____	_____
6.	7.	terminal	8.

B. The word *mediate* has several meanings. Match the dictionary definitions on the left with the example sentences on the right.

> mediate

Definitions

_b_ 1. to try to end a disagreement between two or more people or groups by talking to them and trying to find things they can agree on

___ 2. to succeed in finding a solution to a disagreement between people or groups

___ 3. to influence something or make it possible for it to happen

Example Sentences

a. Innovation is mediated by investment in research.

b. The lawyer is currently mediating the dispute between the two companies.

c. The head officer successfully mediated an agreement between the two agencies.

C. The word *core* has several meanings. Write *a*, *b*, or *c* to show which meaning of *core* is used in each sentence.

a. the hard, central part of a fruit	b. the central part of an object	c. the most important part of something

_b_ 1. The Earth's core is extremely hot.

___ 2. Sander ate the apple and threw away the core.

___ 3. The core reason for the trip was to take time to relax.

___ 4. The generator is located in the core of the building.

___ 5. The core objective of the firm is to find and hire young talent.

D. *Manipulate* means "to control or use something in a skillful way." Match each person on the left with something they might manipulate.

_d_ 1. a scientist   a. clay to make a shape

___ 2. a restaurant manager   b. the lighting to create a relaxing atmosphere

___ 3. a photographer   c. a file to make it easier to download

___ 4. a computer programmer   d. data to present it in a clear format

___ 5. a small child   e. a photo to make it look more colorful

E. Cross out the word or phrase in parentheses that has a different meaning from the others. Use a dictionary to help you understand new words.

1. The mining team used the two technological approaches (*simultaneously / together / successively / concurrently*).

2. After the update was installed, the program was (*ended / stopped / terminated / released*).

3. Nowadays communication is a (*positive / core / principal / main*) part of medical education.

4. Elena (*denoted / marked / initiated / represented*) important information from the lecture by drawing a star next to it in her notes.

5. Through several experiments, the scientist was able to (*reach a conclusion on / deduce / determine / admit*) the cause of the phenomenon.

6. The lawyer (*worked to resolve / mediated / tried to settle / added to*) the disagreement between the company and its employees.

About the Topic

Papua is a province in Indonesia. It is home to many different tribes. A tribe is a group of people consisting of families that share the same customs and language. In recent years, Papua's population has grown. This increase is partly due to migration, in which people from other parts of the country have come to live in Papua.

Before You Listen

Read these questions. Discuss your answers in a small group.

1. What are some unique aspects of your culture?

2. What cultural customs outside of your own culture do you find interesting?

3. How important is it for a culture to preserve its customs and traditions?

Listen

Read the Listen for Main Ideas activity below. Go online to listen to a discussion between two research journalists and their project manager. They have just returned from Papua in Indonesia.

Listen for Main Ideas

Mark each sentence as *T* (true) or *F* (false). Work with a partner. Restate false sentences to make them correct.

_T_ 1. The findings from Papua are going to be included in a seminar.

___ 2. The tribe builds large houses at the bottom of trees.

___ 3. One reason to build the tree houses is for protection against mosquitos.

___ 4. The tribe's population is increasing.

___ 5. The tribe's language is colorful and descriptive.

PRESENTATION SKILL   Deductive and Inductive Reasoning

LEARN

Deductive reasoning means that you start with a general hypothesis or statement. Next, you test to see if the statement is true by making observations, collecting information, and analyzing data.

Sample hypothesis: *The tribe's main source of calories is sago.*

Sample observation: *In a study of food consumed by 138 families across three towns, we found that the greatest source of calories per week was sago.*

Inductive reasoning means that you start with a specific observation. Then using the observation, you try to form a general statement.

Sample specific observation: *Sago is the main source of calories for one family in the tribe.*

Sample generalization: *It is likely that sago is the main source of calories for the entire tribe.*

Scientifically, deductive reasoning is considered a more reliable method for proving something. However, inductive reasoning can help you to develop a general statement that can be tested by using deductive methods, so it is also a useful form of reasoning.

APPLY

A. Go online and listen to the discussion again. Complete the thoughts in the notes section in the chart below.

Student notes	(D / I)
Anders, disc. why Korowai build tree houses: another tribe built homes in trees 4 protection; so *thought they built tree houses 4 protection, too*	*I*
Tian, disc. Korowai tribe's popltn: · some sci's hypothesized → that tribe's popltn _____ · evidence → intrv'd tribal elders ab. parents, brothers, sisters, family · made popltn _____ · studied current popltn · popltn _____ slightly from 20 yrs ago	
Tian, disc. Korowai migration: · met a couple men = moved 2 town 2 work · _____ → the decline	

B. What type of reasoning do the notes in each row of the chart above demonstrate? In the right-hand column, mark each row of notes as either *D* (deductive reasoning) or *I* (inductive reasoning).

C. Discuss with a partner: *How would you use deductive reasoning to form a conclusion about the following statement?*

A university degree is more valuable than a high school degree.

D. Discuss with a partner: *How would you use inductive reasoning to form a conclusion about the statement in activity C?*

E. Which type of reasoning is more persuasive: deductive or inductive? Explain your answer to your partner and listen as your partner also explains his / her answer.

LEARN

English speakers stress some words to bring attention to them in a sentence. You can do this when you speak to highlight differences and correct misunderstandings. This type of sentence focus is called *contrastive stress*.

A. Go online to listen to a conversation. Notice how the speakers shift the stress to draw attention to contrasting elements.

Conversation	Stress	Sentence focus and meaning
A: A good diet includes a variety of vegetables, whole grains, and lean protein.	normal	highlights new information
B: But a healthy diet doesn't include any fat, right?	special	contrasts parallel elements
A: Actually, eating fat from **PLANTS** is part of a healthy diet.	EXTRA	corrects inaccurate information

APPLY

A. Go online to listen. Speaker A uses contrastive stress to highlight very specific information. Circle the word that sounds slower, higher, and more meaningful than the other words in each sentence.

1. (Good) nutrition includes a variety of vitamin-rich foods.

2. Good nutrition includes a variety of vitamin-rich foods.

3. Good nutrition includes a variety of vitamin-rich foods.

4. Good nutrition includes a variety of vitamin-rich foods.

5. Good nutrition includes a variety of vitamin-rich foods.

B. Listen to the conversation. Number the sentences below to show the correct sequence. Notice the contrastive stress used to correct information.

____ A: In certain cultures it's considered impolite to refuse any food.

____ B: Oh, I see. In some cultures, it's polite to accept the food and OK to not finish it.

____ B: Are you saying, in some cultures, you are supposed to eat everything on your plate?

____ A: You got it.

____ A: Actually, you don't have to eat it. But it's polite to say yes to all offers of food.

____ A: No, leaving food on your plate is fine.

____ B: So, it's impolite to leave food on your plate?

C. Go online to listen to the conversation from activity B again. Repeat what you hear. Match the speed, stress, and intonation. Then practice with a partner.

D. Work in a group of three. Partner 1: Read a statement from the left column of the chart below. Use normal sentence focus. Partners 2 and 3: Choose a response and give extra stress to contrasting elements. Partner 1: Listen to your partners' responses. Repeat your statement. Use exaggerated stress to make your meaning clear.

*P1: I booked an expensive cruise to Bali. P2: A **cheap** cruise? P1: I booked an **EXPENSIVE** cruise to Bali. P3: To **Mali**?*

	Sample statements	Sample responses
1.	Michael booked an expensive cruise to Bali.	Michelle did? / He canceled one? / A cheap cruise? / He booked a flight? / To Mali?
2.	He came in on the first flight from New York.	She did? / He left? / On the last flight? / On the first train? / To New York? / From Las Vegas?
3.	Pete will be singing at a café this Friday night.	Paul will? / He might be? / He'll be waiting tables? / On a street corner? / Next Friday night? / Saturday night? / Friday afternoon?
4.	I caught the 8:30 morning bus to San Francisco.	Your friend did? / You missed it? / The 9:30? / The 8:45? / The evening bus? / The morning train? From San Francisco? / To Las Vegas?

End of Unit Task

In this unit, you learned about synthesizing key information and concepts. Additionally, you learned about identifying and using inductive and deductive reasoning. Apply these skills as you complete the following activities.

A. Think of a cultural group that you are interested in or know about. Working with a partner, record two customs or cultural practices of this group.

1. _____

2. _____

B. Try to determine the meaning or reason behind the customs and cultural practices that you noted in activity A? Use deductive and inductive reasoning.

Deductive reasoning	Inductive reasoning
1.	1.
2.	2.

C. Take turns discussing, with a partner, the customs or cultural practices of the group that you selected.

1. As you listen to your partner, take notes on the key information that you hear in the left column of the chart below.

2. After listening to your partner, use the key information that you heard to write down two related concepts in the chart.

3. Discuss your concepts with your partner. Working with your partner, add one more concept to the chart below.

Key information	Related concepts
	1.
	2.
	3.

D. With your partner, choose one concept from your chart and synthesize it by describing its importance or your opinion of it.

Synthesis

E. Share the ideas and information that you synthesized with your partner.

F. Using your notes, share your key information, concepts, and synthesis with the rest of the class.

Self-Assessment		
Yes	No	
☐	☐	I listened to and synthesized information from a lecture.
☐	☐	I was able to identify and use deductive reasoning.
☐	☐	I was able to identify and use inductive reasoning.
☐	☐	I can use stress to highlight differences and correct misunderstandings while speaking.
☐	☐	I can correctly use the target vocabulary words from the unit.

Discussion Questions

With a partner or in a small group, discuss the following questions.

1. What is the best way to deal with a cross-cultural misunderstanding?

2. How would you describe your culture to someone who is unfamiliar with it?

3. In what ways might the field of anthropology benefit society?

The Academic Word List

Words targeted in Level 4 are bold

Word	Sublist	Location
abandon	8	L2, U4
abstract	6	L3, U3
academy	5	L2, U10
access	4	L0, U5
accommodate	9	L3, U6
accompany	**8**	**L4, U2**
accumulate	8	L3, U4
accurate	6	L0, U2
achieve	2	L0, U4
acknowledge	6	L0, U7
acquire	2	L3, U9
adapt	7	L3, U7
adequate	4	L3, U9
adjacent	**10**	**L4, U4**
adjust	**5**	**L4, U4**
administrate	**2**	**L4, U8**
adult	7	L0, U10
advocate	**7**	**L4, U3**
affect	2	L1, U1
aggregate	**6**	**L4, U6**
aid	7	L0, U5
albeit	**10**	**L4, U3**
allocate	6	L3, U6
alter	5	L2, U6
alternative	3	L1, U1
ambiguous	**8**	**L4, U7**
amend	**5**	**L4, U7**
analogy	**9**	**L4, U1**
analyze	1	L1, U3
annual	4	L1, U9
anticipate	9	L2, U8
apparent	4	L2, U4
append	**8**	**L4, U10**
appreciate	8	L0, U9
approach	1	L1, U1
appropriate	2	L3, U5
approximate	4	L2, U7
arbitrary	**8**	**L4, U7**
area	1	L3, U7
aspect	2	L2, U7
assemble	10	L3, U1
assess	1	L2, U8
assign	6	L3, U5
assist	2	L0, U2
assume	1	L3, U1
assure	**9**	**L4, U8**
attach	6	L0, U10

Word	Sublist	Location
attain	9	L3, U5
attitude	4	L2, U4
attribute	4	L3, U8
author	6	L0, U1
authority	1	L2, U2
automate	8	L2, U1
available	1	L0, U8
aware	5	L1, U1
behalf	**9**	**L4, U9**
benefit	1	L1, U2
bias	**8**	**L4, U3**
bond	**6**	**L4, U9**
brief	6	L2, U9
bulk	9	L3, U1
capable	6	L3, U5
capacity	5	L3, U2
category	2	L2, U4
cease	9	L2, U2
challenge	5	L1, U6
channel	**7**	**L4, U5**
chapter	2	L0, U2
chart	8	L0, U2
chemical	7	L2, U6
circumstance	**3**	**L4, U2**
cite	**6**	**L4, U4**
civil	4	L3, U2
clarify	8	L3, U7
classic	7	L3, U6
clause	**5**	**L4, U8**
code	4	L0, U5
coherent	**9**	**L4, U7**
coincide	**9**	**L4, U10**
collapse	10	L3, U9
colleague	10	L1, U5
commence	9	L2, U4
comment	3	L1, U4
commission	2	L3, U2
commit	4	L2, U1
commodity	**8**	**L4, U4**
communicate	4	L1, U3
community	2	L1, U4
compatible	9	L2, U4
compensate	**3**	**L4, U8**
compile	**10**	**L4, U9**
complement	**8**	**L4, U8**

Oxford 3000™ words

Word	Sublist	Location		Word	Sublist	Location
complex	2	L2, U1		currency	8	L2, U3
component	3	L3, U1		cycle	4	L3, U5
compound	5	L3, U10				
comprehensive	7	L2, U6		data	1	L0, U4
comprise	7	L3, U7		debate	4	L3, U5
compute	2	L1, U8		decade	7	L1, U9
conceive	**10**	**L4, U7**		decline	5	L1, U9
concentrate	4	L1, U5		**deduce**	**3**	**L4, U10**
concept	1	L3, U10		define	1	L0, U8
conclude	2	L0, U6		**definite**	**7**	**L4, U8**
concurrent	**9**	**L4, U10**		demonstrate	3	L1, U2
conduct	2	L1, U4		**denote**	**8**	**L4, U10**
confer	**4**	**L4, U8**		deny	7	L1, U8
confine	**9**	**L4, U8**		depress	10	L0, U8
confirm	7	L1, U8		**derive**	**1**	**L4, U8**
conflict	5	L1, U7		design	2	L0, U10
conform	8	L3, U6		despite	4	L3, U6
consent	3	L3, U3		detect	8	L2, U3
consequent	**2**	**L4, U2**		**deviate**	**8**	**L4, U10**
considerable	**3**	**L4, U1**		device	9	L0, U2
consist	1	L1, U9		devote	9	L2, U3
constant	3	L1, U8		differentiate	7	L3, U6
constitute	**1**	**L4, U5**		**dimension**	**4**	**L4, U9**
constrain	**3**	**L4, U6**		diminish	9	L2, U8
construct	2	L3, U1		**discrete**	**5**	**L4, U2**
consult	5	L2, U8		**discriminate**	**6**	**L4, U5**
consume	2	L2, U6		displace	8	L3, U10
contact	5	L1, U4		display	6	L0, U8
contemporary	**8**	**L4, U6**		**dispose**	**7**	**L4, U1**
context	1	L2, U4		**distinct**	**2**	**L4, U2**
contract	1	L3, U4		**distort**	**9**	**L4, U5**
contradict	8	L2, U4		distribute	1	L1, U9
contrary	7	L3, U1		diverse	6	L3, U2
contrast	4	L3, U2		document	3	L0, U4
contribute	3	L1, U9		**domain**	**6**	**L4, U6**
controversy	9	L2, U9		domestic	4	L2, U5
convene	**3**	**L4, U1**		dominate	3	L3, U7
converse	9	L2, U2		draft	5	L0, U10
convert	7	L3, U3		drama	8	L2, U9
convince	10	L1, U5		duration	9	L2, U3
cooperate	6	L3, U6		dynamic	7	L3, U3
coordinate	3	L2, U2				
core	**3**	**L4, U10**		economy	1	L2, U8
corporate	3	L1, U7		edit	6	L1, U7
correspond	3	L2, U10		element	2	L3, U1
couple	7	L0, U4		eliminate	7	L1, U6
create	1	L3, U7		emerge	4	L3, U5
credit	2	L2, U7		emphasis	3	L1, U5
criteria	3	L3, U2		**empirical**	**7**	**L4, U4**
crucial	8	L3, U7		enable	5	L2, U1
culture	2	L0, U10		encounter	10	L1, U8

Oxford 3000™ words

Word	Sublist	Location		Word	Sublist	Location
energy	5	L0, U9		function	1	L3, U3
enforce	**5**	**L4, U1**		fund	3	L2, U5
enhance	6	L3, U2		fundamental	5	L1, U8
enormous	10	L0, U7		furthermore	6	L3, U4
ensure	**3**	**L4, U1**				
entity	**5**	**L4, U8**		gender	6	L3, U8
environment	1	L1, U1		generate	5	L1, U5
equate	2	L3, U10		generation	5	L2, U10
equip	7	L2, U1		globe	7	L2, U5
equivalent	5	L1, U7		goal	4	L0, U7
erode	**9**	**L4, U2**		grade	7	L0, U3
error	4	L0, U2		grant	4	L3, U9
establish	1	L2, U5		guarantee	7	L1, U7
estate	**6**	**L4, U8**		guideline	8	L1, U6
estimate	1	L2, U5				
ethic	9	L3, U4		hence	4	L3, U6
ethnic	4	L3, U9		**hierarchy**	**7**	**L4, U6**
evaluate	2	L1, U8		highlight	8	L0, U7
eventual	8	L3, U2		hypothesis	4	L3, U4
evident	1	L2, U8				
evolve	5	L2, U2		identical	7	L3, U3
exceed	6	L1, U10		identify	1	L1, U3
exclude	3	L3, U8		**ideology**	**7**	**L4, U3**
exhibit	8	L2, U3		ignorance	6	L2, U9
expand	5	L0, U5		illustrate	3	L0, U1
expert	6	L0, U3		image	5	L1, U3
explicit	**6**	**L4, U3**		**immigrate**	**3**	**L4, U7**
exploit	**8**	**L4, U9**		impact	2	L2, U9
export	**1**	**L4, U6**		**implement**	**4**	**L4, U2**
expose	**5**	**L4, U1**		**implicate**	**4**	**L4, U3**
external	5	L2, U1		**implicit**	**8**	**L4, U3**
extract	7	L3, U1		imply	3	L3, U8
				impose	4	L3, U10
facilitate	5	L3, U6		**incentive**	**6**	**L4, U2**
factor	1	L3, U1		incidence	6	L3, U4
feature	2	L0, U2		**incline**	**10**	**L4, U4**
federal	**6**	**L4, U4**		income	1	L0, U4
fee	6	L0, U5		**incorporate**	**6**	**L4, U9**
file	7	L0, U5		**index**	**6**	**L4, U9**
final	2	L0, U1		indicate	1	L2, U10
finance	1	L3, U6		individual	1	L0, U1
finite	**7**	**L4, U9**		**induce**	**8**	**L4, U1**
flexible	6	L1, U10		inevitable	8	L3, U2
fluctuate	**8**	**L4, U10**		**infer**	**7**	**L4, U3**
focus	2	L0, U6		**infrastructure**	**8**	**L4, U1**
format	9	L2, U8		**inherent**	**9**	**L4, U7**
formula	1	L3, U5		**inhibit**	**6**	**L4, U2**
forthcoming	**10**	**L4, U10**		initial	3	L0, U3
found	9	L0, U7		initiate	6	L3, U8
foundation	7	L1, U9		**injure**	**2**	**L4, U9**
framework	**3**	**L4, U6**		innovate	7	L3, U1

Word	Sublist	Location
input	6	L2, U5
insert	7	L2, U7
insight	9	L3, U4
🔑 inspect	**8**	**L4, U9**
🔑 instance	3	L3, U3
🔑 institute	2	L1, U6
instruct	6	L1, U6
integral	**9**	**L4, U6**
integrate	**4**	**L4, U6**
integrity	10	L2, U1
🔑 intelligence	6	L0, U10
🔑 intense	8	L3, U7
interact	3	L2, U3
intermediate	9	L2, U5
🔑 internal	4	L1, U10
interpret	1	L3, U10
🔑 interval	6	L3, U10
intervene	7	L3, U6
intrinsic	**10**	**L4, U7**
🔑 invest	2	L3, U2
🔑 investigate	4	L2, U9
invoke	**10**	**L4, U5**
🔑 involve	1	L3, U7
isolate	7	L3, U2
🔑 issue	1	L0, U3
🔑 item	2	L0, U6
🔑 job	4	L0, U10
journal	2	L1, U10
🔑 **justify**	**3**	**L4, U2**
🔑 label	4	L0, U1
🔑 labor	1	L2, U4
🔑 layer	3	L3, U3
🔑 lecture	6	L0, U6
🔑 legal	1	L1, U2
legislate	**1**	**L4, U1**
levy	**10**	**L4, U3**
🔑 **liberal**	**5**	**L4, U3**
🔑 license	5	L3, U8
likewise	10	L3, U4
🔑 link	3	L0, U4
🔑 locate	3	L1, U4
🔑 logic	5	L3, U5
🔑 maintain	2	L1, U10
🔑 major	1	L3, U7
manipulate	**8**	**L4, U10**
manual	9	L3, U10
margin	5	L2, U3
mature	9	L2, U8

Word	Sublist	Location
maximize	3	L1, U9
mechanism	4	L3, U3
🔑 media	7	L0, U8
mediate	**9**	**L4, U10**
🔑 medical	5	L1, U2
🔑 medium	9	L1, U10
🔑 mental	5	L2, U6
🔑 method	1	L1, U2
migrate	**6**	**L4, U1**
🔑 military	9	L2, U3
minimal	9	L1, U9
minimize	8	L3, U1
🔑 minimum	6	L1, U10
🔑 **ministry**	**6**	**L4, U6**
🔑 minor	3	L0, U7
mode	**7**	**L4, U5**
modify	5	L1, U6
🔑 monitor	5	L3, U4
motive	6	L2, U7
mutual	9	L2, U2
negate	**3**	**L4, U4**
🔑 network	5	L2, U2
neutral	6	L2, U5
🔑 nevertheless	6	L3, U5
nonetheless	**10**	**L4, U5**
norm	**9**	**L4, U7**
🔑 normal	2	L0, U6
🔑 notion	5	L3, U5
notwithstanding	**10**	**L4, U6**
🔑 nuclear	8	L3, U9
🔑 objective	5	L0, U4
🔑 obtain	2	L3, U4
🔑 obvious	4	L1, U7
🔑 **occupy**	**4**	**L4, U8**
🔑 occur	1	L2, U10
🔑 odd	10	L1, U8
offset	**8**	**L4, U9**
ongoing	10	L2, U7
🔑 option	4	L1, U10
orient	**5**	**L4, U4**
outcome	3	L2, U7
🔑 output	4	L2, U5
🔑 overall	4	L2, U9
overlap	9	L2, U4
🔑 overseas	6	L2, U3
🔑 **panel**	**10**	**L4, U5**
paradigm	**7**	**L4, U2**
paragraph	8	L1, U7

🔑 Oxford 3000™ words

Word	Sublist	Location
parallel	4	L4, U3
parameter	4	L3, U4
participate	2	L1, U2
partner	3	L0, U3
passive	9	L3, U10
perceive	2	L3, U7
percent	1	L1, U3
period	1	L3, U3
persist	10	L3, U4
perspective	5	L2, U10
phase	4	L2, U10
phenomenon	7	L4, U4
philosophy	3	L3, U8
physical	3	L0, U1
plus	8	L0, U6
policy	1	L2, U9
portion	9	L2, U6
pose	10	L4, U4
positive	2	L0, U7
potential	2	L2, U10
practitioner	8	L4, U1
precede	6	L3, U9
precise	5	L3, U3
predict	4	L0, U9
predominant	8	L4, U5
preliminary	9	L2, U2
presume	6	L4, U7
previous	2	L0, U9
primary	2	L1, U3
prime	5	L4, U2
principal	4	L2, U10
principle	1	L3, U10
prior	4	L2, U8
priority	7	L2, U6
proceed	1	L2, U1
process	1	L1, U2
professional	4	L1, U2
prohibit	7	L3, U2
project	4	L1, U9
promote	4	L4, U7
proportion	3	L2, U8
prospect	8	L4, U6
protocol	9	L4, U9
psychology	5	L2, U8
publication	7	L3, U9
publish	3	L0, U1
purchase	2	L0, U7
pursue	5	L4, U4
qualitative	9	L4, U8
quote	7	L1, U7

Word	Sublist	Location
radical	8	L4, U5
random	8	L2, U5
range	2	L2, U10
ratio	5	L3, U10
rational	6	L3, U9
react	3	L1, U3
recover	6	L2, U1
refine	9	L3, U5
regime	4	L3, U9
region	2	L2, U2
register	3	L3, U8
regulate	2	L2, U2
reinforce	8	L3, U4
reject	5	L1, U10
relax	9	L0, U6
release	7	L2, U5
relevant	2	L3, U8
reluctant	10	L2, U3
rely	3	L2, U9
remove	3	L0, U9
require	1	L0, U10
research	1	L0, U3
reside	2	L4, U3
resolve	4	L2, U4
resource	2	L0, U3
respond	1	L1, U4
restore	8	L2, U10
restrain	9	L3, U9
restrict	2	L2, U7
retain	4	L4, U7
reveal	6	L2, U1
revenue	5	L3, U6
reverse	7	L3, U9
revise	8	L1, U7
revolution	9	L3, U3
rigid	9	L2, U6
role	1	L0, U9
route	9	L3, U9
scenario	9	L2, U7
schedule	7	L1, U5
scheme	3	L3, U2
scope	6	L2, U9
section	1	L0, U9
sector	1	L4, U6
secure	2	L1, U6
seek	2	L2, U7
select	2	L1, U4
sequence	3	L1, U6
series	4	L0, U9
sex	3	L4, U4

Oxford 3000™ words

Word	Sublist	Location
shift	3	L2, U7
significant	1	L3, U2
similar	1	L1, U5
simulate	7	L3, U4
site	2	L0, U5
so-called	10	L2, U9
sole	**7**	**L4, U10**
somewhat	7	L3, U7
source	1	L1, U1
specific	1	L1, U6
specify	3	L1, U8
sphere	**9**	**L4, U6**
stable	5	L3, U10
statistic	4	L3, U8
status	4	L0, U4
straightforward	10	L3, U6
strategy	2	L2, U2
stress	4	L3, U7
structure	1	L2, U1
style	5	L2, U2
submit	7	L1, U10
subordinate	**9**	**L4, U3**
subsequent	4	L3, U5
subsidy	**6**	**L4, U8**
substitute	5	L2, U3
successor	7	L3, U6
sufficient	**3**	**L4, U2**
sum	4	L3, U9
summary	4	L1, U3
supplement	9	L2, U6
survey	2	L2, U6
survive	7	L2, U9
suspend	**9**	**L4, U5**
sustain	5	L3, U1
symbol	5	L0, U8
tape	6	L3, U8
target	5	L2, U6
task	3	L0, U5
team	9	L0, U3
technical	3	L3, U3
technique	3	L3, U5
technology	3	L2, U10
temporary	9	L0, U8
tense	7	L2, U6
terminate	**7**	**L4, U10**
text	2	L0, U1
theme	7	L1, U5
theory	1	L3, U8
thereby	**7**	**L4, U7**
thesis	**7**	**L4, U7**

Word	Sublist	Location
topic	7	L0, U6
trace	**6**	**L4, U5**
tradition	2	L0, U2
transfer	2	L1, U6
transform	6	L3, U1
transit	5	L2, U8
transmit	**7**	**L4, U1**
transport	6	L1, U1
trend	5	L1, U4
trigger	**9**	**L4, U1**
ultimate	7	L3, U8
undergo	**10**	**L4, U9**
underlie	**6**	**L4, U5**
undertake	**4**	**L4, U2**
uniform	7	L2, U4
unify	9	L2, U5
unique	7	L3, U10
utilize	6	L3, U1
valid	3	L3, U8
vary	1	L2, U1
vehicle	7	L1, U1
version	5	L1, U7
via	**7**	**L4, U4**
violate	**9**	**L4, U3**
virtual	8	L3, U3
visible	7	L2, U6
vision	9	L0, U8
visual	8	L3, U7
volume	3	L1, U8
voluntary	7	L3, U10
welfare	**5**	**L4, U9**
whereas	**5**	**L4, U5**
whereby	**10**	**L4, U10**
widespread	7	L2, U3

Oxford 3000™ words